.

Nicole Dake

MillenialMom

CONTENTS

CONTENTS

1 |

Introduction:

This book is about learning to live your best life, by reducing stress in typical problem areas. This includes our health, our relationships, and our finances. When we are stressed, we are unhappy, and we become short tempered, making those around us unhappy as well.

Many of us are so stressed out at times that we inadvertently make choices that, while aimed at reducing our stress level, can increase our stress. This can include overindulging in things like fast food, coffee, and alcohol. Or, staying up late to catch up on work or schoolwork. Or we may engage in "retail therapy" by shopping excessively to cope with stress and find that our budget is suffering.

Learning better coping mechanisms, including good health behaviors, better communication and financial planning can help us to reduce our stress levels. Some of these same habits can help us go from barely surviving to thriving.

Something you will see about me as you go through this book is that I am a mystical soul with an analytical mind. You will notice threads of spirituality and mysticism interwoven with facts. Life is made up of both.

We experience life both in the mind and in the world.

The intent of this book is to help you improve both aspects of your life. When we improve something in either our inner world or our outer world, it ends up improving both.

I am happier now because of a combination of improving my mindset, my health, my relationships, and my financial situation. It is hard to say which had the biggest impact, but I believe they all flow together.

As you address your own goals, focus on your personal priorities and realize that improving one aspect of your life will improve them all. It is just a matter of deciding what you will work on first.

How I got here.

Are you unhappy and struggling to admit it to yourself? Or does your life feel stagnant, like you are living on autopilot? I felt that way too. Outwardly, everything in my life was fine. But 'fine' didn't feel like it was enough. I wanted things to be good. I had needs swimming below the surface that were unfulfilled.

My family wasn't exactly struggling, but we were just maintaining the status quo. Our income was just enough to pay our bills, but never enough to get ahead. My partner was working long hours at a job he didn't like, just so we could pay some minimal bills and keep our toddler in daycare. It felt like all we were doing was working, and not enjoying our time as a family enough because we were always too tired.

I felt like we were working too hard and sacrificing too much to be going nowhere. I felt like there had to be a better way to get through life, so I made the goal planner contained in this book for myself to take a deeper look at my life and what was important to me.

Using this goal setting process, I started to ask myself some hard questions. I asked myself:

What do I really want?

What makes me happy?

What does my perfect life look like?

How can I downsize to stop worrying about money?

When I went through this process, I didn't do it alone. I talked things through with my partner, at every step of the way. We tossed around ideas about how to change our lives for the better. We wanted to go from surviving to thriving.

Of course, the easiest thing to do would be just to wait, do nothing, and maintain a life that was fine.

Or we could take our daughter out of daycare and one of us could have stayed home with her, stretching our budget even thinner.

For a while, we also seriously debated selling everything and moving to the country on a farm. We looked at properties, priced it all out, and watched a bunch of videos about homesteading. Ultimately, we went in another direction, and were able to refinance our mortgage to get costs down.

Along the way, I did some therapy and took an intensive 12-week mindset coaching program. At the start of the program, my coach asked me my goals. I told her I wanted to find inner peace. I felt like, if I could get my mindset under control, I would then be able to fix everything else. She told me it sounded doable, and I found inner peace by week four. Mind you, inner peace doesn't immediately fix all your problems, you must do that yourself.

Finding inner peace creates a space for happiness.

Both peace and happiness came to me through practicing yoga, mindfulness, and learning to slow down and appreciate the little things in life.

It seems difficult to find happiness when we are stuck in daily worries and stress.

The goal of this book is to help you reduce stress and find tools to create happiness. This can be done by building new habits to reduce stress and create happiness at the same time. It also involves breaking out of old habits that are not working. Sometimes, we get these habits from our parents, or do things because that is just the way it has always been done.

The problem with some of the habits formed that way, though, is that in our parent's generation, success was more important than happiness. Our parents thought it was perfectly normal to work a 40-, 50- or 60-hour week every week, go out on the weekend to the bar on Friday nights to unwind, and then shamble back sadly to a job they hated on Monday morning.

Our generation craves work-life balance and wants to experience happiness in life as most countries have done in Europe for a long time now, instead of just surviving to face another day. We feel a hollowness in the lifestyle that we learned from our parents in some cases and yearn for something more.

It may seem that, as stress goes down, happiness will automatically go up. This isn't really the case. We need to consciously build good habits to replace the bad, otherwise, we just end up empty.

Happiness is more than just the absence of pain.

Happiness comes from adding good things to our lives, not just taking away the bad. You won't be happy if you starve yourself to lose weight or if you stop spending any money on fun to pay down debt. Change like that just creates an emptiness of bad, not the presence of good.

When we try to change by just taking things away, our lives become empty. Then, typically we will go back to our old habits because they are all that we know.

To create lasting, positive change, we need to fill up the empty space with something good. That is why this book takes a twofold approach to both reduce stress and create happiness.

Happiness

All the aspects of our lives are interconnected, and when one of them isn't going well, then it can put our whole life wildly out of balance. Creating happiness is in large part about creating balance.

Happiness can mean many things to many different people. If you are happy you are typically living in the moment and enjoy what you are doing. This enjoyment can take many different forms. You may enjoy spending time with friends and loved ones, doing a hobby, practicing self-care, traveling, learning a new skill, or having a meaningful career. For most people, happiness is some combination of all these things.

Think about a time when you were the happiest. Remember it in detail. Who were you with? What were you doing? Think about all the sights, smells, and sounds around you. Immerse yourself in that moment. Then, think about which of those things truly makes you happy.

Change can be one of the hardest things for us to tackle because many of us are not programmed to do so. Entertain the possibility to try something new you never dared to do. For instance, try learning a new skill such as a foreign language, cooking for example or simply change things up by going for a daily walk or reading a book. You never know what talents might be hidden inside you that can bring out happiness.

Describe your happiest time.

2

Living Your Best Life.

When we learn to live our best life, it makes us happier. Remember then, that happiness is about choice. There is a series of small choices that we make every day that can make us happier. We can find ways to choose things that are good for ourselves physically, mentally, and socially. To be happier, we say yes to the things that we love, things that feed our souls, and 'no' to things that are not serving our good.

Think about the memory you just described, and all the things that make you happy. As you read through this book, I invite you to think about how you can incorporate some of those qualities of what happiness means to you into your daily life.

One of the problems we have in our society is that we think we must wait to be happy. We think that we will be happy when we get a new job, new house, new TV, or go on that trip. And while that may be true, it is unfortunate to make happiness contingent on something in the future. We can choose to incorporate happiness into our daily habits and routine, so that happiness isn't something in the future, it is something that we experience every day. Old sayings like "Stop to smell the flowers" or "It's the journey and not the destination" is a kind of wisdom that have endured through the times for a reason.

Earlier this year, I was feeling very directionless and spent a lot of time thinking about what living my best life would really look like. That is partially how this book came into being. The goal planning steps that I am giving you throughout, and my advice on how to live your best life come from my own experiences in finding happiness.

In this book, we will talk a lot about different habits that can reduce our stress and make us happier.

Remember, as you build new healthy habits, and replace old ones, go slowly. When you try to make big sweeping changes all at once, they are not sustainable. That's why new year's resolutions do not work. You are trying to change too much all at once.

My recommendation for you would be to choose one small habit in each category to start with. These categories are, one thing for your physical health, one thing for your mental health, and one thing for your social-emotional health.

It is a great idea to set long-term goals for where you want to be. Envision your perfect life, and then slowly forge the way to get there. You can do that by setting daily, weekly, and monthly goals to get there.

If your goal is to eat healthier for example, decide that today you will eat one piece of fruit instead of one piece of candy. Do that for a week. Then, next week, eat two pieces of fruit instead of two pieces of candy. Don't try to go vegan, gluten free and stop sugar all at once. You are going to crash and burn. When you make small goals and succeed, you are setting a strong foundation for yourself to build on. In a world where everyone is in a hurry. Remember, good change takes time and will likely last longer.

You may also want to do some journaling, introspection, and talking to your partner about what your long-term goals are. As you move forward, you will be building a healthier, happier life for yourself and your family with a strong foundation. As you decrease the causes of stress in your life, you can increase the sources of happiness. But do both at the same time. Don't just try to get rid of things that you don't want. When it comes to habits, you need something else to fill the space. Otherwise, it is too easy to go back to our previous habits. I hope that you have the most beautiful life, full of happiness and peace.

Happier Mom = Happier Kids.

When we are unhappy, our kids can tell. And since they think the world revolves around them, they often will self-blame for parental unhappiness. Have you heard of couples divorcing and kids blaming themselves? Even if your problems aren't to that point, it is the same principle.

Being healthier makes us happier. Being happier makes our kids happier. And you know what else? Happier kids listen better and do what they are supposed to do more easily! So, working on your own happiness is a win-win-win!

Kids can teach us happiness too.

How is that? Because kids live perpetually in the moment. They are completely absorbed with whatever they are doing. It may be looking at a beautiful butterfly, or petting a cat, or drawing a picture. In any case, they become completely present and focused on what is at hand. They don't worry about what is coming next. They don't understand time or money. They live in a perpetual, exciting NOW.

Being present is a key component of Mindfulness, which we will talk about later! And it is something our kids intuitively already know how to do. This is one area to take a page out of your kids play book. Spend some time each day playing with the kids and be fully immersed in what you are doing. Let them lead the way and follow along with their fun!

Kids are all about having fun, and guess what? Fun makes us happier!

Going through the process of
setting and meeting goals can
make you happier.

As we go through this book, there will be workbook pages to fill out
that talk about goal setting. When you are reading through each topic,
there will also be journal pages to fill out where you can take some time
to think about how the topics impact you personally. While you are
thinking about how the things in your life is working or not working,

you can visualize what could make your life better. No matter how good our lives are, we can always work toward constant improvement.

Setting goals is something I have always done personally, possibly since I am a driven individual. But goals can be helpful for everyone. They help us focus our energy on the direction that we want to go. Often, when we are directionless, that is when we flounder, and find ourselves under the most stress. Once we decide where we are going, it is much easier to get there.

Deciding about what we want from life can be our guide. Do you want to start a business? Travel? Buy a new house? Any of those are great goals, and there are so many more. When we decide what we want to do, we can make a plan to make our dreams come true.

How do you know what your best life is? Visualize in your mind your perfect life. What does it look like? What kind of person do you want to be? Think about it in your mind and use the next page to write about your perfect life.

My Perfect Life:
_____

Priorities and Values: Why they matter with kids.

The first step toward setting goals is to choose your priorities and decide what is important to you. If you try to do everything, you are bound to fail. So, it is important to choose a few areas to focus on so that you are able to excel.

Goals with your kids.

Have you ever heard the saying that "You have to pick your battles?" Well, this is especially true with kids. I have a toddler that asks me to do something about every 5 minutes, and it can be anything from kissing an owie, to playing a game, or getting some candy. Some of these I say yes, some I say no, and for a while I would get irritated about how often she would ask me something.

It's easy to let any little issue turn into a big argument. Over time, I have had to learn to pick my battles with my kids. Am I happy when my daughter wipes play dough on the carpet? Or when she dumps a whole jar of fish food into the tank? Not really. But I am re-learning to let some things slide.

Figuring out your priorities.

When my now-teen daughter was little, I decided that the three things I wanted more than anything else for her to do were:

1. Eating Healthy
2. Doing Well in School
3. Getting Along with Others

Now that she has graduated from High School with high marks, I think for the most part, she has internalized the things that I think are important.

Most of all, what I want for my kids is for them to be healthy and happy.

I grew up in an authoritarian household, where I constantly was afraid of what my parents thought of me. Happy kids is something that I have always strived for. That means, I try to encourage my children in the direction they are going and help them get there the best they can. I don't try to direct their course.

When my children take up an interest, like cosplay, building, or art, I try to get interested in it with them and help them to get better at their hobbies or interests.

Personal Values.

Values are ideas and beliefs that are important to us. In many ways, our values shape our reality, because they determine the way we live our lives. Many times, we are unaware of our value system, and we can have conflicting values taking us in separate directions. When we are trying to go two different directions, we end up going nowhere fast.

Many people adopt a value system from religion or culture from an early age. If this is the case for you, then your values may be deeply ingrained in your subconscious, and not something you spend time thinking about daily.

Self-awareness or self-realization is the first step before you can make plans. Too often our subconscious is guided by our childhood and parents. While we rebel often in our teenage years to defy the things we do not want to do and actively change ourselves, later in life we often fall right back into duplicates of our parents – for better or worse.

Let me give you an example and while it may not apply to your life it should certainly make you understand what I am trying to convey.

A friend of mine in her late 40's suddenly became aware that everything he did for the better part of her life was to follow the path her mother laid out for her. As mothers so often do, hers applied a heavy pressure to succeed. There is nothing wrong with that in itself. But it takes a life of its own when the child adopts a drive for success it without the knowledge to distinguish between the mother's goal and their own. Success can be a good income or personal gratification in what we do, perfect success is both. It took her the better part of her life to realize that everything she did was her mother's wishes and, in the end, failed in both. She was never truly happy.

What we can take away from this is that we sometimes, or often, do things in our lives that we are certain who we are. Motions we go through that define us are not necessarily who we really are.

When we take our values from religion, often they are the values handed down to us from our parents and grandparents. If we attend religious services from a young age, we grow up with religious stories that teach moral behaviors and ideas about right and wrong.

Examples of religious value systems would be the 10 Commandments in Christianity, or the 4 Noble Truths in Buddhism.

Cultural values are beliefs that are held by most people in a country or culture. In the US, many of the beliefs and values that we practice daily are laid out in the Constitution.

Some examples of US cultural values would include the ideas of freedom, equality, and the pursuit of happiness.

To some extent, we all have values shaped by religious and cultural norms that we have grown up with. However, at times there are cultural shifts in society, such as gay marriage or the Black Lives Matter movement, which may cause us to reconsider our values and belief system.

Also, our values may change somewhat as we move through different phases of life. For example, when you are a high school or college student you may value individuality and autonomy the most, but when you become a parent then you start to value family more.

Earlier this year, I took a class with my work where we were asked to pick out our top five values from a list. You can brainstorm your own, or you can look at this *list*.

We all most likely have more than five values in life, the idea is to choose which values are most important to you in your current phase of life. This is also an exercise that you can do with children or teens, although with very young children I have rephrased the question to "what makes you happy" instead of "what are your values" since happiness is a more accessible concept for small children.

To give you an example of what I am talking about, here are my top five values:

1. Trust
2. Honesty
3. Kindness
4. Family
5. Safety

As a mom, I incorporate these values in both the way I treat my kids, and the way I teach my kids to interact with the world.

For example, I think that if I treat my kids with honesty and kindness, they will learn to trust in me, which allows them to feel safe.

When I was younger, I was out of touch with my values. I spent all my time working (away from my family) to make money. If I value family higher than money, it makes sense for me to take more time with my kids, and less time at work. You could argue instead though, that if I use the money to provide my kids a better life, that all the time at work was well spent.

There are no right or wrong values. We just want to be sure that we are organizing our lives in a way that allows us to pursue what is most important to us. For instance, if you really want to be a marine biologist, then we want to take classes about biology and whales, not classes about business management. Make sense?

Now that you have read a bit about values, write a little bit about what your personal values are.

My Personal Values:

5

Following Our Values in an Intentional Way

When we become aware of our values, that allows us to set goals that align with what is most important to us. Intentional, goal directed action allows us to live life to the fullest because we are living life in a way that we have chosen.

A life guided by values, priorities and goals allows us to have a sense of purpose about the things that we do. It also allows us to devote our time, energy and efforts in a way that is going to make us feel fulfilled.

As moms, we are probably some of the busiest people out there. There are always 20 things that need to be done, some of them immediately, some of them yesterday, and some of them that your toddler asked you for in the last five minutes.

It basically goes without saying that there are going to be things left undone at the end of the day, almost every day. By aligning our goals and our actions to our priorities and values, we can ensure that *the most important things* are getting done each day. So, we didn't scrub the grout on the bathroom floor with bleach today. It isn't going to kill us if it waits for tomorrow.

The cool thing is, we each get to decide for ourselves, each day, what the most important things are.

When I set goals, I have big overarching life goals, but I split them into smaller goals on a daily, weekly, and monthly basis.

With our kids, it is important to teach them about the world in such a way that we allow them to choose their own priorities and values as they grow up and feel safe to be themselves with us. There are many ways to do this, by teaching them as much about the world as we can in a non-judgmental way.

Helping Kids Choose Their Own Priorities.

When kids are young, helping them choose their priorities may mean having them choose between band and volleyball as an afterschool club, what color to paint their room, or what vegetable to have with dinner. For the bigger decisions, you can have them do something like a pro's and con's list and talk through the decision.

With my kids, I let them know that whatever choice they make, I will support them.

As they get older, the choices will get more complicated. When they get ready for college, choosing a major will be something difficult that they will all experience. If they are lucky, during high school they will be able to experiment with different fields of study and find out what they like.

Before she decided on what to major in, I told my daughter to go on *www.glassdoor.com* to look up information about different jobs. I told her to look at the jobs she might want, and what locations she could find the highest paid job in that field. Or, if there was somewhere she specially wanted to live, to find out what the highest paid jobs were. One strategy places the career first, the other location first. So, it depends on which is a higher priority to each child.

Expose Kids to Varied Experiences.

In order to help kids find out what their priorities and values are, it may help to expose them to many different types of experiences. The more they know about the world, the better equipped they will be to make informed decisions that will serve them well in the long run.

One way to do this is by taking them to the library and exposing them to different types of books. I always like letting my girls browse through shelves of books, reading stories with them, and fostering learning.

When my oldest was in 3rd grade, she wanted to learn about every different type of insects. Each week, we would go to the library and check out a book about a different insect to take home. Then, when she got older, she volunteered at the Butterfly Pavilion, a local attraction for schools and families to learn about insects, spiders, fish and yes, butterflies. I don't know anything about bugs, but she was fascinated, and I helped her pursue her interest.

You can also expose your kids to varied experiences through travel. Going to new places, learning about new cultures, and eating different foods can also broaden kids' horizons. Showing them that there are many ways of living life shows them that they have a wide range of options.

Along with travel, we can expose our kids to learning foreign languages. Often, when kids learn new languages, they can also learn about other countries, and other cultures.

Different cultures often have different value systems, and different ways of living. For example, in Spain, they take a siesta (nap) in the afternoon and businesses close. Many countries in Europe also allow for a month's vacation each year, so travel is much more of an option.

When we provide our children with varied experiences, it allows them to discover their interests and broaden their horizons.

In the Amish culture, teens turn 18 and go out into the city to spend a year abroad before they settle into life (Rumspringen). Mormons go on a mission trip for a year, so that they can see the world as well. Joining the Peace Corps, or a Foreign Exchange program also allows young people to go out into the world in somewhat of a structured way to experience new things away from home prior to choosing college or a profession.

Another option is for teens to join the military after high school and before college. In Israel, all young people are required to serve in the military. This is another type of cultural experience that allows young people to go out into the world and learn new skills.

There are many ways for kids to get out and experience the world before they "settle down" and choose their path. One thing I told my teen daughter when she turned 18 is that being an adult is about being able to make your own choices. Also, just because you have chosen one path, it doesn't mean you are locked in forever. The average person now changes careers 5 times in their lifetime. That creates a freedom in knowing that a choice doesn't have to be forever if it isn't right for you anymore.

The More Intentional We Are, The More Intentional
They Are.

When we model intentional goal-setting behavior in line with our values, the more likely that our kids will do the same. Kids learn more by example than anything else.

Whether they choose 'our' values or not, supporting them along the way will help them to clearly understand what their own values are, and how to pursue them.

Once you or your kids choose the values that are most important to you, then you can set goals that align with your values. To meet those goals, you can make a schedule for your year, month, and day. This can include a morning routine that helps you get excited about what you are going to experience or accomplish.

Setting Goals Lets Us Accomplish More.

Do you ever feel like your life is standing still? Or like you are just treading water, and doing the same things every day? Like your life is going nowhere. I think we all feel that way at times, and personally I notice that it happens to me when I am not setting any goals for myself.

We can't make any kind of progress in life if we don't know where we want to go. I always believe that I can do anything that I set my mind to, so the problem comes in when I have become indecisive and haven't set my mind to anything. I am just doing what needs to get done every day, not making any plans, and have nothing to look forward to.

Times like that, my life has felt stagnant.

When I was in high school, someone told me that, "A goal is a dream with a plan." That has always resonated with me, as someone who is driven to be continuously moving forward.

My oldest daughter just graduated from High School this year, so for the last year I have been trying to think of all the things I wish someone would have told me at that age.

Finally, I told her: "Think about what your dream life would be. Ask yourself, what would be the coolest thing ever? Then, figure out a plan to make it happen."

Dream Big, Plan Small.

It's great to have a big dream as your desired result. Personally, I have always believed that the shortest distance between two points is a straight line. When there is something that I really want, I look at where I want to be. Then I research to figure out the steps to get there. I am here to tell you that no dream is unrealistic.

I grew up in the 80's with my dad always telling me that if you work hard enough, you can achieve anything you set your mind to. That is only the first piece of the puzzle though. First, you paint the big picture. Then, you start breaking down the smaller steps.

Goals for Every Day.

First, we have big, overarching goals of what we want to accomplish with our whole life. This is a vision that I personally set with my partner and in discussion with my family.

I also have personal goals that I want to work on that are just for me. For example, I want to lose the rest of the baby weight from when my 4-year-old was born.

So, I want to lose 20 pounds by the end of the year. That is the big goal.

After I set the big goal, I set little goals for the week to help me get there:

1. Work out for 30 minutes every day.
2. Eat salad for lunch.
3. Drink 80 ounces of water.

The little goals sound much more manageable than the big goal. I work on them every day for the week. Then, then next week I set goals that are going in the same direction but a little bit harder.

Do you see how that works?

Goals for Each Part of My Life

Usually, at any given time, I will be working on multiple different goals to create the life that I want.

Typically, I have a goal for my health and fitness, personal finances, skills I want to build with my kids, and a work goal.

In each of those domains, I set a goal where I would like to be eventually, then I break them down into little goals that I am going to work on every day. Knowing that I have succeeded on a daily goal helps to keep me motivated moving forward toward my larger goals.

If you aren't sure what goals you would like to work towards, it can help to journal about your perfect life, or to make a vision board so that you can visualize what would make you happy.

Making a Vision Board.

Every year, at the beginning of the year, I make a vision board for myself. I go through a big stack of magazines and cut out pictures of things that make me happy, and words that represent what I want for myself. Then, I get a big poster board and organize similar things together and glue them on.

Usually, I have a lot of things I want to do for my kids, and things that I want to do for myself. It is typically things like games and crafts, exercise, the ocean, horses, music, and some travel.

Once I have made my vision board, I will hang it near my work area so that I can be reminded of all the things that I really want from life. That helps me to stay aligned to what I really want instead of going off on tangents. Our most precious resource is our time, and it makes sense to spend time doing the things that we want to do most of all. It helps us to eliminate distractions, and to say no to things that don't align to our vision.

Helping Kids Set Goals.

Teaching kids to set goals is important too. Whether they want to learn to do a handstand or get into college. You can use a similar process to setting your own goals.

You can use a more informal process or help them put their goals down on paper when they get older.

Often with toddlers, it can be helpful to use a chart where you put stars every time they go potty, tie their shoes, or put their toys away. When we teach them to meet goals that you have chosen, it is a stepping-stone to teaching them to set their own goals. It also prepares them for more formal evaluations when they get into school.

Goal Planning Worksheets

As moms, we are busy all the time! That is why it has become so important to me to be intentional about what I prioritize in life, and how I schedule my time.

The idea behind these goal planning worksheets that you will find throughout this book is to help you dream big and be able to plan small. Most people typically are either "big picture" people, or "detail oriented." We are thinkers or doers. So, if we want to learn how to be both, and do so effectively, we will need to step out of our comfort zone a little bit.

I am excited to be able to share this journey with you, and feel free to contact me any time with questions that you may have about this planner or about parenthood in general.

Step 1: Personal Values and Mission Statement

After you read the blog post and watch the video about values, you can go to the link provided for a list of sample values, or you can create your own. Remember there is no right or wrong here! You can also follow along with the examples provided in this guide.

Once you choose your top five values, you can use those values to create your personal mission statement. A mission statement is a statement that explains how you plan to live your life according to your values. Many times, you will see these on company websites. It is a part of branding, and right now you are creating your own personal brand!

When you write your mission statement, write it in the present tense, since this is something that you are committing to doing daily.

Example:

My personal values are:

- Trust
- Family
- Stability
- Kindness (compassion)
- Growth

My mission statement is: "I *trust* myself and my partner to make *compassionate* decisions that allow us to create *a stable* home environment for our *family*, which enables us to *grow*."

When I wrote this mission statement, I reworded it several times before I was finally happy with it. Similarly, you can write out your mission statement, sit with it for a few days, and see if it still resonates with you.

This planner can help to create an introspective process that allows you to be in touch with your inner thoughts and allow the things that are truly important to you to direct your life.

My mission statement is:

Work Goals

If you don't work, you can change this to a different category that makes sense for you. It resonates with me as a working mom, and I spend quite a lot of time working between my day job and blogging. I haven't written a specific type of work that I will do here on the cover sheet. The overarching work goal is like the mission statement you put on your resume.

Your work goal can outline the type of work that you want to do, for example if you want to be a teacher, doctor, or chef. It can also specify if you want to work from home, what your salary expectations are, or whatever is most important to you about your career.

If you want to obtain a job in a different location, you can put that here too!

Example:

My work goals are: "I do meaningful work in a collaborative and respectful workplace."

For me, the type of work that I do is not as important as the type of people that I work with. Collaboration and respect are values that are important to me on the job and help me to work effectively.

Another example would be: "I want a teaching job in Chicago, working with children in second grade math."

Think about what is most important to you about the work that you do. Are you like me, and value working with nice people? Do you want work/life balance? Do you want a certain salary? Do you want health insurance? Do you want to telework? Do you want an office with windows?

The possibilities are endless! Think about what is most important to you, and then write that down. Remember, there are no right or wrong answers here! This planner is all about finding what makes you happy and makes your life work.

My Work Goal:

It may seem a little bit weird to some of you that I have put affirmations on this page. I find, though, that saying daily affirmations helps me to dream big. Creating a positive mindset through affirmations allows me to believe in myself, and my dreams, and keep going forward no matter what obstacles may stand in my way.

Example:

My daily affirmations include:

- I love and accept myself.
- I am a good person.
- I am worthy of love.
- I am kind and gentle to myself.
- I matter.
- What I want matters.
- Opportunities come to me easily.

Over time, the affirmations that I use daily change, based on what areas of my life that I am working on. If there are struggles that I am trying to overcome, typically, I will try to say an affirmation every day to contradict my negative thinking.

For example, if I am struggling every day and saying to myself, "I am a bad mom." Or "I am always late." Some affirmations I would use for myself would be, "I am a good mom." and "It is easy for me to be on time." Of course, affirmations don't solve all our problems, they are just one skill that we have in our toolbox to create a great life for ourselves.

My Daily Affirmations:

Section 2: Life Goals

This page can be used to outline your long-term life goals. To figure out your life goals, you can ask yourself, "what would be the perfect life?" You can also talk with your partner about what you see yourselves doing in the future. This is like that question they always ask in job interviews, "Where do you see yourself in five years?"

To figure this part out, you can also do journaling, or create a vision board. I do both of those myself. With the vision board, like we discussed at the beginning of the chapter. If you aren't crafty, you can make your vision board on Pinterest too.

Example:

My life goals are:

- Complete a mindset coaching program.
- Trust myself and my decisions.
- Rework my toddler's nighttime routine.
- Pay down credit cards.
- Lose weight.
- Stop smoking.?
- Become a blogger full time.

My work goal, I listed the same as on the first page, since it is an overarching goal of what I want to do with my career. You can do the same thing too, or you can break down your goal and get more specific.

Family Goals:

These can be goals that you want to work on with your partner and your kids. It would be things like, getting a child into a better bedtime routine, or homework routine.

Example:

I want to get my toddler to go to bed earlier and with less stress and argument.

Action Steps:

Action steps are the steps that we will take to meet each goal that we have set in the previous sections. Our Life Goals are lofty and pie in the sky. But action steps are more concrete and allow us to make a plan for how we are going to make our goals real and achievable.

In the planner, the action steps are broken out into sections similarly to the Life goals page. If you notice, each page that you move forward, you are continuously getting more specific with what you are going to do. You are narrowing your focus from the big picture down to the little details.

Example:

When it comes to my personal goals, I will take losing weight as an example, since that is a goal that many of us share.

Action steps for losing weight include:

- Spend 30 minutes exercising each day.
- Burn 500 active calories per day.
- Take a multivitamin to lower cortisol (a stress hormone that also makes you retain fat)
- Eat a healthy diet with more servings of vegetables and protein.
- Eat less snacks, especially chocolate.

Action steps are still somewhat general, but they are much more concrete than our life goals.

Weekly Goals:

This is where we start to get specific on what needs to be done. We may want to only set 1-2 goals in each section. I'm going to continue with my example on losing weight for the next two examples.

Example:

Spend 30 minutes exercising each day

- I will wake up at 6am every day and do 30 minutes of yoga first thing.

Burn 500 active calories:

- I will make sure to get up from my desk for a few minutes every hour.
- I will go for a swim or a walk during my lunch break.
- I will play an active game with my toddler after daycare.

I will take a Multivitamin

- I will take a vitamin first thing in the morning, after I do yoga, when I am getting my first cup of coffee. (My vitamin case is right next to the coffee pot – makes it hard to forget!)

Eat a healthy diet with more servings of vegetables and protein.

- I will drink a protein smoothie each day for breakfast.
- I will eat a healthy dinner, not fast food.

Eat less snacks, especially chocolate

- I will eat a fruit or vegetable if I am wanting a snack.
- I will limit myself to one piece of chocolate per sitting.

Daily Goals:

Daily goals are smaller still and more specific. You can set them for yourself either first thing in the morning, or the night before. Typically, I do this for myself at the end of my workday before I pick up my toddler from daycare.

As you can see, with weekly goals we broke down our action steps. With our daily goals we break it down even more.

Example:

With the weight loss goal, I would try to break up some of the little steps across different days. For example, on Sundays I fill up my vitamin container for the week, so that I have my vitamins easily at hand on my workdays. On Mondays I go grocery shopping, and make sure that I buy healthy food (and no chocolate!). Typically, the rest of my week I do all the same things (my daily routine!).

I will discuss setting up a daily routine and schedule in later chapters. Having a routine allows us to do something predictable each day, and make sure that we are going to do all the things that are most important to us each day as part of a routine.

On Saturday or Sunday, I could go for a hike, bike ride, or spend the day at the pool to work on my fitness goal.

Since we have many different goals, I might work on one goal on Monday, another on Tuesday, etc. When I fill out my daily goals and schedule, that allows me to further prioritize each task relating to my goals, along with any other tasks that may need to be done. Like if my daughter is in the school play or needs to go to soccer practice. That probably is not the day I want to be shopping, meal planning, or balancing my checkbook.

Example 2:

Now I am going to take my goal of paying down credit cards (since that is also common to most people) and walk-through Action Steps, Weekly and Daily Goals.

Action Steps:

- Make all payments on time
- Figure out how to lower payments
- Make extra payments

Weekly Goals:

- Make my credit card payments.
- Call my credit card company to ask if I can get a lower interest rate
- Set aside $10 in savings to put toward credit card payments.

Daily Goals:

- Monday – pay my credit card payment
- Tuesday – look up my interest rate
- Wednesday – call credit card company
- Thursday – talk to my partner about the call with credit card company
- Friday – decide next steps
- Saturday – put $10 into savings

Hopefully that helps you understand the process of getting more and more specific with your goals. If you look at my daily goals with the credit card example, I am doing one task to meet my goal each day. The tasks also flow in a logical order.

With the Friday goal of deciding next steps, I could set my weekly goals for the following week each time. When we have large goals, they may seem very daunting when we stare at our "Life goals" page. It may be hard to decide where to start.

One thing I have learned, even if you don't start with the "right" task, it is important just to get started. Once you take a couple of steps, you can re-adjust your course.

When I started paying down my credit cards, I looked at filing bankruptcy. I realized very quickly that I don't qualify for that and I started researching other things that I could do.

The great thing about setting big goals, and then planning small steps, is that often we find the small steps don't work. At that point we can either give up and say the goal is stupid, or we can just set a different small goal for the next day or week.

No matter what your goals are, there is a way to meet them, it just comes down to finding your way.

In the following pages, you can use the goal planning charts to write out your own goals. You can fill them out now, or as you read through each chapter and find things that resonate with you.

Mission and Values

Personal Values and Mission Statement:

Work Goals:

Affirmations:

Life Goals

Personal Goals:

Work Goals:

Family Goals:

Action Steps

Personal Goals:

Work Goals:

Family Goals:

Weekly Goals

Personal Goals:

Work Goals:

Family Goals:

Daily Goals

Personal Goals:

Work Goals:

Family Goals:

Mission and Values

Personal Values and Mission Statement:

Work Goals:

Affirmations:

Life Goals

Personal Goals:

Work Goals:

Family Goals:

Action Steps

Personal Goals:

Work Goals:

Family Goals:

Weekly Goals

Personal Goals:

Work Goals:

Family Goals:

Daily Goals

Personal Goals:

Work Goals:

Family Goals:

Mission and Values

Personal Values and Mission Statement:

Work Goals:

Affirmations:

Life Goals

Personal Goals:

Work Goals:

Family Goals:

Action Steps

Personal Goals:

Work Goals:

Family Goals:

Weekly Goals

Personal Goals:

Work Goals:

Family Goals:

Daily Goals

Personal Goals:

Work Goals:

Family Goals:

6

Negative Impacts of Stress

Small amounts of stress are not bad and can actually push us towards achievement. For example, if you are stressed about a deadline at work, it can push you to get a good work product done faster. However, it is the effects of chronic stress over time that can have many toxic effects on our health and on our life.

According to the Mayo Clinic, stress can impact us by causing any of the following effects on your body, mood and behavior:

- Headache
- AnxietyOvereating or undereating
- Muscle tension or pain
- Restlessness
- Angry outbursts
- Chest pain
- Lack of motivation or focus
- Drug or alcohol misuse
- FatigueFeeling overwhelmed
- Tobacco use
- Change in sex drive
- Irritability or anger
- Social withdrawal
- Stomach upset

- Sadness or depression
- Exercising less often
- Sleep problems

If these symptoms are left untreated for long periods of time, they can lead to chronic health problems with some serious consequences. According to the National Institute of Mental Health,

> *"Coping with the impact of chronic stress can be challenging. Because the source of long-term stress is more constant than acute stress, the body never receives a clear signal to return to normal functioning. With chronic stress, those same lifesaving reactions in the body can disturb the immune, digestive, cardiovascular, sleep, and reproductive systems. Some people may experience mainly digestive symptoms, while others may have headaches, sleeplessness, sadness, anger, or irritability.*
>
> *Over time, continued strain on your body from stress may contribute to serious health problems, such as heart disease, high blood pressure, diabetes, and other illnesses, including mental disorders such as depression or anxiety."*

Since chronic stress can have such potentially catastrophic effects on our health, it is important to mitigate our life stress as soon as possible. That is what we will be discussing in this section of the book. In the following chapters I will discuss how to reduce stress in many areas of your life that typically causes the highest amount of stress.

Common Causes of Stress

In the United States, the leading causes of stress, according to Very Well Mind are:

1. Financial Problems
2. Work
3. Personal Relationships

4. Parenting
5. Daily life and busyness

Throughout this book, I will discuss how to deal with different types of stressors including: financial stressors, relationships, and reducing how busy you are through better scheduling. As you reduce stress in these typical problem areas, you free up your mental resources to do things that make you happier and more fulfilled. This is how we live our best life.

As you read through this book, think about your main causes of stress, and what your goals are for both reducing stress and creating happiness. The two processes go hand in hand. Reducing stress can make us happier and being happier can reduce our stress. As you think about stressful habits that you want to break, also start thinking about positive habits that you can replace them with.

Coping With Stress as a Mom

I love being a mom, and I love my kids. They give me a sense of purpose in what I do. But along with all the good parts of being a mom, there is a lot of stress too. Some of it is personal, like not getting enough sleep or time for self-care. Other stress can come from constantly having to clean up messes, paying bills, finding childcare, working, taking care of the house, and worrying if we are being good parents to our children.

We may ask ourselves questions like:

- Why isn't my baby sleeping?
- Why does my toddler always say no?
- Am I doing enough to help my child learn?
- When am I going to have time to clean?
- How am I going to afford what my child needs?
- Do I listen well enough?
- Is it OK for my child to have screen time?

- What kind of family activities can we do?
- Why am I always tired?
- How can I lose the baby weight?
- Should I go back to work?
- Can I work from home?
- Is my child meeting milestones on time?
- How can I get my child to eat vegetables?

The list of worries we have as mothers goes on seemingly endlessly. We all want our children to have the best in life, but sometimes it is hard to know what that is. We try to strike a balance between providing our children with love and attention and working to make money to provide for their needs. And somewhere in there, we are supposed to make time for self-care, exercise, proper sleep, and maintaining closeness with our partners.

Even at the best of times, life can be stressful, but if you are experiencing any type of difficult life events, it can be even more so. As moms, we are expected to be superwomen balancing family, career, social life, our own health, and so much more. It can seem overwhelming to manage everything sometimes. Hopefully as we continue throughout this book, you can learn some skills to lessen the stressors of everyday life through goal planning, scheduling, and rethinking the way you organize your life.

Experiencing any type of life changes can be very stressful, so can a lack of support system, being a single mother, losing a job, moving a house, and so many other things. With this added amount of stress, life can quickly go from difficult to impossible. That makes planning even more important. Sometimes it can help to see a therapist if the pressure becomes unbearable. Having a listening ear always helps.

As we learn to manage our stressors better, it can help us to be better moms too.

7

Wellness can combat stress.

When we are at our best physically, mentally, and socially, we are better able to cope with life's stress and to be calm moms. We can engage with our children and be fully present with them when we play together. This makes maintaining our own health a priority because it benefits our kids as well.

According to the University of Minnesota,

"Even if you cannot remove the source of stress from your life, you can take steps to react to it in healthy, positive ways.

Stress is deeply related to and intertwined with various aspects of your wellbeing; it affects and is affected by many lifestyle choices you make. Chronic stress can make it very challenging to effectively address addictive and unhealthy behaviors, such as overeating, drinking too much alcohol, smoking, and skipping exercise routines. This creates a problematic loop, because these behaviors then cause more stress!"

Basically, when we are tired and stressed, we tend to turn to maladaptive coping strategies, like eating too much chocolate, smoking, drinking, or binge-watching Netflix all night. These things in turn impact our health and make our stress even worse than it was before.

Have you ever sat up late into the night worrying about all the things you have to do the next day? Then, when the morning rolls around, you are exhausted and drink 13 cups of coffee, eat a box of donuts, and feel no motivation at all to complete any of your to-do list items?

Then, other days you have a peaceful night of sleep, wake up early and do yoga and journaling, and feel refreshed and ready to start the day?

Good health behaviors make us feel better and reduce our stress levels.

According to University of Minnesota, here are some activities that can boost wellness and reduce stress:

- Physical Activity and Fitness
- Diet and Nutrition
- Thoughts and Emotions
- Sleep
- Purpose
- Relationships
- Community
- Environment
- Security

By taking control of our wellness in these areas, we can drastically reduce our stress and be able to be happier moms. Also remember that if you implement these types of good health, stress relieving behaviors with your kids, they will be able to develop more resilience to help them cope throughout life.

8

Types of Wellness

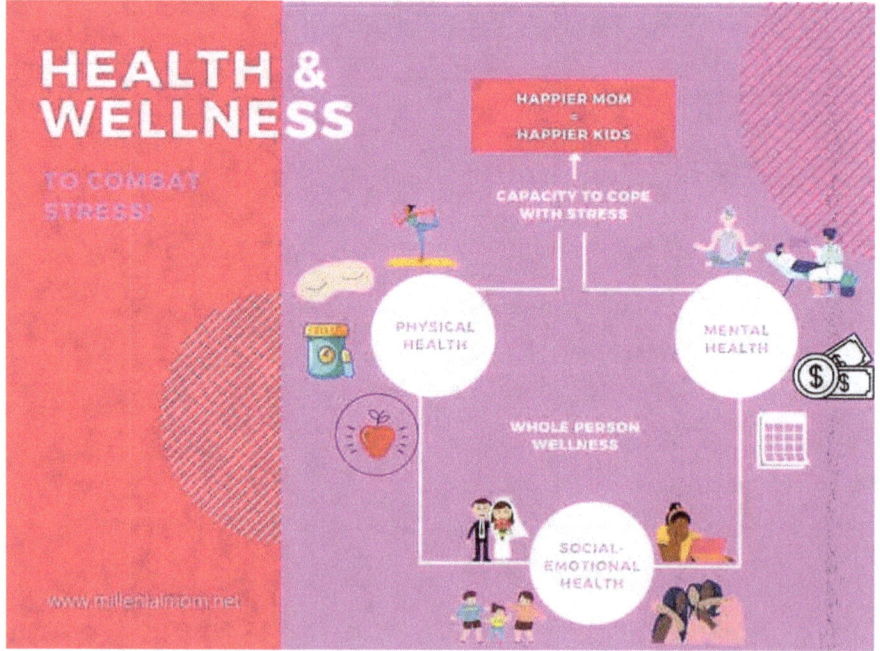

When I think of wellness and stress relief, I think of physical health, mental health, and social-emotional health. All these domains of wellness are things you can work on for yourself as well as your kids.

The following chapters outline some strategies that you can use to reduce stress and improve your health in each of these areas of your life. Although some of these activities are categorized under physical or mental health, it is important to realize that all areas of our health are intertwined. So, that may mean that something like sleep can impact both our physical and mental health. Keep that in mind as you are reading through the different health behaviors in each category; many of them fit into more than one aspect of our overall health.

9

Physical Health

Our physical health is one of the main determinants of our happiness (or unhappiness) in life. If you have ever been sick, you probably realize the truth of this. When we are sick we often describe ourselves as feeling "miserable." Being miserable is about as far as possible from being happy.

In addition to illness, we spend time worrying about our weight, our wrinkles, whether we are getting enough exercise, and many other things.

Research has found that being happier can make us healthier and, conversely, that being healthier makes us happier. According to Pritikin, "Being physically active causes chemical changes in the brain which can help improve your mood. It also brings a sense of greater self-esteem. An analysis of 36 studies found a strong relationship between physical activity and mental wellness."

Also, Harvard Health says, "Want to feel better and improve your health? Start by focusing on the things that bring you happiness. Scientific evidence suggests that positive emotions can help make life longer and healthier. But fleeting positive emotions aren't enough. Lowering your stress levels over a period of years with a positive outlook and relaxation techniques could reduce your risk of health problems."

It makes sense then, to start by focusing on our physical health and the health-happiness connection.

Get Regular Medical Care

The first step to maintaining your physical health is to get regular medical care and preventative care doctor checkups. You have probably heard the old saying, "an ounce of prevention is worth a pound of cure." Well, when it comes to getting regular medical treatment, that is extremely true. It is important to get regular health screenings from your doctor, dentist, and eye doctor. When you get regular checkups and preventative care, it is easier to prevent many serious health conditions, or at least to catch them early when they are more easily treatable.

Having a primary care doctor, vs. just using emergency or urgent care, also allows you to work with the same medical provider all the time. That way, your medical provider can get to know you and your medical history and will be better able to treat any illness that you are experiencing.

The same is true for the dentist and the eye doctor. Getting your preventative care on a regular basis can prevent the need for costly and invasive surgeries down the line.

According to Health for California, "Preventive care can help keep you healthy longer by preventing or delaying the onset of diseases. Preventive care can also help you save you money because you won't have to treat a costly illness. If you want to make your health a priority, learning about and using preventive care is a great place to start."

Get enough sleep.

Another important aspect of maintaining your physical health is making sure that you get enough sleep each night. Getting enough sleep each night can have a huge impact on your health, your energy level, your mood, and more. When we are tired, we are less motivated, and more likely to consume too much caffeine, which creates a vicious cycle of not sleeping well again the next night.

How much sleep do you need?

It is recommended by the Mayo Clinic that you get at least 7 hours of sleep per night. The Mayo Clinic also cautions that, "For adults, getting less than seven hours of sleep a night on a regular basis has been linked with poor health, including weight gain, having a body mass index of 30 or higher, diabetes, high blood pressure, heart disease, stroke, and depression."

Causes of Poor Sleep

Getting enough sleep each night can be a challenge in our busy world, especially if you have a baby. I know everyone says sleep when the baby sleeps, but you can do that even until toddler age to make sure you are well rested. (I still nap when my 4-year-old does, and go to bed at the same time.) Eventually your child will learn to sleep better, and this can improve your sleep too. If your child's sleeplessness is contributing to problems for you, be sure to talk to their pediatrician, and to your own doctor.

Also, avoid looking at your phone right before bed, it can be over stimulating and increase your stress level. According to Clinic Cleveland, there are three reasons why checking your phone right before bed can cause poorer sleep: It keeps your mind psychologically engaged, the blue light from the screen suppresses melatonin, and the alerting properties delay REM sleep. Clinic Cleveland, "recommends to cut off screen time 1 hour before bed, but says there are even benefits to discontinuing it just 30 minutes before bed. And sure, smart phones are typically the main culprit, but even tablets and TVs can emit blue light that can contribute to poor sleep."

If it is hard for you to disconnect from your phone, you can always put your phone onto night mode, and have all your notifications automatically turn off. Some phones have sleep settings so that you can set up your typical sleeping schedule, and it will even automatically notify you to turn your phone off to wind down. To relax before bed, you can try reading a book, journaling, doing yoga or progressive muscle relaxation instead. Or, have a cup of warm tea and write down your to-do list items for the next day to prepare. Perhaps set yourself with boundaries. Take away the underlying stress of always having to be available after a certain time at night.

Another cause of poor sleep is staying up later at night to get things done that you didn't during the day. Once you are well rested in the morning, you will be able to get more done. According to Facile Things, "The first thing you do when you can't achieve as much as you planned in a day is to cut on sleep. Thus, you receive a few extra hours to focus on work. Here's the paradox: sleeping less is precisely what leads you to poor work performance and decreased productivity during the day. So, by sleeping less you don't help yourself at all." When we try to push through and get more done, we are being less efficient, and getting less done.

When we are chronically sleep deprived, according to Facile Things, it can cause harm to our productivity in several ways: learning and concentration problems, increased stress, weight gain, depression, creativity impairment, and a weakened immune system. All these factors mean that we aren't going to accomplish tasks as quickly. The moral of the story? Don't stay up that extra hour at night trying to finish something. It is going to take longer, and your work probably won't be as good of quality anyway.

Insomnia

All the previous reasons for lack of sleep have to do with your habits. But what if you have insomnia, a medical condition that causes poor sleep, and prevents you from getting proper sleep?

According to WebMD, there are many different causes of Insomnia. "Primary causes of insomnia include:

- Stress related to big life events, like a job loss or change, the death of a loved one, divorce, or moving
- Things around you like noise, light, or temperature
- Changes to your sleep schedule like jet lag, a new shift at work, or bad habits you picked up when you had other sleep problems
- Your genes. Research has found that a tendency for insomnia may run in families.

Secondary causes of insomnia include:

- Mental health issues like depression and anxiety
- Medications for colds, allergies, depression, high blood pressure, and asthma.
- Pain or discomfort at night
- Caffeine, tobacco, or alcohol use, as well as use of illicit drugs.
- Hyperthyroidism and other endocrine problems
- Other sleep disorders, like sleep apnea or restless legs syndrome
- Pregnancy
- Alzheimer's disease and other types of dementia
- ADHD
- PMS and menopause"

If you can't sleep due to insomnia caused by of any of the secondary causes of insomnia, it may be important to treat the primary condition so that you can improve your sleep as well. You may also need to take sleeping pills for a short amount of time to reset your sleep schedule, try taking herbal remedies like melatonin, or see a therapist to uncover the reason for your sleeplessness.

Web MD also advises, "Good sleep habits, also called sleep hygiene, can help you beat insomnia. Here are some tips:

- Go to sleep at the same time each night and get up at the same time each morning. Try not to take naps during the day, because they may make you less sleepy at night.
- Don't use phones or e-books before bed. Their light can make it harder to fall asleep.
- Avoid caffeine, nicotine, and alcohol late in the day. Caffeine and nicotine are stimulants and can keep you from falling asleep. Alcohol can make you wake up in the middle of the night and hurt your sleep quality.
- Get regular exercise. Try not to work out close to bedtime, because it may make it hard to fall asleep. Experts suggest exercising at least 3 to 4 hours before bed.
- Don't eat a heavy meal late in the day. But a light snack before bedtime may help you sleep.
- Make your bedroom comfortable: dark, quiet, and not too warm or too cold. If light is a problem, use a sleeping mask. To cover up sounds, try earplugs, a fan, or a white noise machine.
- Follow a routine to relax before bed. Read a book, listen to music, or take a bath.
- Don't use your bed for anything other than sleep and sex.
- If you can't fall asleep and aren't drowsy, get up and do something calming, like reading until you feel sleepy.
- If you tend to lie awake and worry about things, make a to-do list before you go to bed. This may help you put your concerns aside for the night."

Eat a balanced diet.

The next aspect of maintaining our physical health is eating a balanced diet. For me, this is the hardest part of maintaining my health. It is just so easy to throw a pizza in the oven and not worry about dinner. If you are like me and hate to cook, try cutting up fresh fruits and veggies to have available throughout the day for snacks. That can help round out your diet and stop from eating too much junk food!

Take a Multivitamin

Taking a multivitamin can help you to get added vitamins that may be missing in your diet. According to UT Southwestern Medical Center, "According to the Dietary Guidelines for Americans 2020-2025, American diets often lack calcium, vitamin D, potassium, and fiber. Most multivitamins contain 100% of the daily value for vitamin D but have limited amounts of calcium and potassium and no fiber." You can take additional vitamins to make up for those deficits and be sure to eat foods that contain those vitamins.

Studies have shown differing results on whether you actually need to take a multivitamin, but if you are taking them, it is good to be sure to take one that is tailored to your age group. These days, there are specific vitamins for children, women, men and seniors. My doctor recommended that for a woman of child-bearing age, it is good to always take prenatal vitamins, even if you don't plan to become pregnant. That is because of the additional calcium and iron in prenatal vitamins, which can help with a woman's health.

MyPlate Nutrition Guidelines

There are many different diet fads out there, and they have good and bad points. I am not going to go into specifics of any of those here. If you have specific dietary needs, it is best to consult with your doctor or a nutritionist.

The My Plate Nutrition Guidelines have replaced the Food Pyramid that we all grew up learning about as children in the last few years. These are the new US guidelines on getting proper nutrition, based on current science. By following these guidelines, you should be able to maintain a healthy diet and get proper nutrition.

According to eMedecine Health, "MyPlate is based on nutrition advice from the government's 2010 Dietary Guidelines for Americans. It is a graphic representation of plate, quartered into sections, where half the plate is comprised of fruits and vegetables:

• Fruits

- Any fruit or 100% fruit juice
- May be fresh, canned, frozen, or dried
- The amount each person needs can vary between 1 to 2 cups each day
- Vegetables
  - Any vegetable or 100% vegetable juice
  - May be raw or cooked; fresh, frozen, canned, or dried/dehydrated
  - The amount each person needs can vary between 1 to 3 cups each day
- Grains
  - Foods made from wheat, rice, oats, cornmeal, barley or another cereal grain
    - Examples include: bread, pasta, oatmeal, breakfast cereals, tortillas, and grits
  - The amount each person needs can vary between 3 to 8 ounce-equivalents each day
  - Grains are divided into 2 subgroups:
    - Whole grains
      - At least half the grains consumed should be whole grains
    - Refined grains
- Protein
  - All foods made from meat, poultry, seafood, beans and peas, eggs, processed soy products, nuts, and seeds
  - The amount each person needs can vary between 2 to 6½ ounce-equivalents each day
- A smaller circle appears next to the plate that represents dairy.
- All milk and milk products
- Foods made from milk that retain their calcium content are part of the group
- Foods made from milk that have little to no calcium, such as cream cheese, cream, and butter, are not included

- Calcium-fortified soymilk (soy beverage) is also part of the dairy group
- The amount each person needs can vary between 2 to 3 cups each day

Oils should be consumed in moderation. Avoid trans fats."

To make sure that you are eating the right amounts of each food group every day, you can create a meal plan or sign up for a food subscription box that does all of the math and serving sizes for you. Meal planning is a more cost-effective way to go and allows you to choose your own recipes. Getting a food box subscription is more for if you aren't savvy in the kitchen, and they have some good recipes too.

Also, there are many different apps that you can get for your Smartphone that will help you track your eating and maintain a balanced diet. When I was trying to lose weight a few years ago I used "My Fitness Pal" which is a free app that lets you scan barcodes on boxed food, and type in recipes that you eat frequently to save into the app. It will tell you nutrition information, and how many calories you are eating. There are a variety of these apps on the market that you can try if you are feeling like you need some additional help with your eating habits.

Drink Enough Water

Drinking enough water is important because dehydration can deeply impact our health as well. It is commonly recommended that adults drink 64 ounces of water per day (that is 8, 8oz glasses). If you live in a dry climate, are pregnant or nursing, or have some other health conditions, you may need to drink more.

If you are looking for an easy health habit to start with first, drinking enough water may be your best bet.

According to Healthline, here are seven of the top health benefits of drinking more water:

- Helps maximize your physical performance
- Significantly affects energy levels and brain function
- May help prevent and treat headaches
- May help relieve constipation
- May help treat kidney stones
- Helps prevent hangovers
- Can aid weight loss

Since drinking water has many benefits, and really no drawbacks, increasing your water intake is a great way to make yourself healthier and happier on a daily basis! If you don't like drinking water because of the plain taste, you can try drinking mineral water, or water with a slice of lemon.

Take a Probiotic Supplement

According to Cleveland Clinic, "Probiotics are made of good live bacteria and/or yeasts that naturally live in your body. You constantly have both good and bad bacteria in your body. When you get an infection, there's more bad bacteria, knocking your system out of balance. Good bacteria can help eliminate bad bacteria, returning the balance. Probiotic-supplements are a way to add good bacteria to your body."

Typically, probiotic supplements are supposed to help with digestion. The supplements are supposed to make up for a lack in your body's natural production. It is like taking a multi-vitamin, or other vitamin supplements. Probiotics can be found in yogurt, smoothies, or pill form.

Also, mental health is linked to gut health. According to Healthline, about 95% of the Serotonin (the body's happiness chemical) is produced in your gut. If you are like me, you probably thought it came from your brain, but no! So, just taking a probiotic can improve both your digestion and your mood!

Get proper exercise.

The next aspect of maintaining our physical health is to get proper exercise each day. In order to stay in good health, the Mayo Clinic recommends, "aim for at least 30 minutes of moderate physical activity every day. If you want to lose weight, maintain weight loss, or meet specific fitness goals, you may need to exercise more."

There are many great forms of exercise that can benefit your health, such as lifting weights, Pilates, yoga, swimming, running, walking, rowing, and much more. Here, I am going to discuss the benefits of yoga and walking, since neither one requires any equipment, and you can get started right away. If neither of these appeals to you and you do not want to get any equipment right away, you may want to try body weight exercises (think sit-ups and push-ups) instead.

If you are like many people, and dislike to exercise, you may want to try a group fitness class or going to a personal trainer. That way, you can get some social time during your workout and increase your motivation through accountability.

Walking for Fitness

You can take your baby on a walk.

There are many other benefits of walking for fitness.

Health Benefits of Walking.

According to the Victoria Department of Health,

> *"You carry your own body weight when you walk. This is known as weight-bearing exercise. Some of the benefits include:*

- *increased cardiovascular and pulmonary (heart and lung) fitness*
- *reduced risk of heart disease and stroke*
- *improved management of conditions such as hypertension (high blood pressure), high cholesterol, joint and muscular pain or stiffness, and diabetes*
- *stronger bones and improved balance*
- *increased muscle strength and endurance*
- *reduced body fat."*

Walking is a great exercise for anyone because it is low-impact, and something that you can easily incorporate into your day with no equipment needed.

Mental Health Benefits.

In addition to the physical benefits of walking, it can also have mental health benefits. According to WebMD, "walking regularly can help ease symptoms related to chronic mental health conditions like anxiety and depression."

Some of the mental health benefits you can experience, according to WebMD, include:

- Improved sleep
- Better endurance
- Stress relief

- Improvement in mood
- Increased energy and stamina
- Reduced tiredness that can increase mental alertness
- Weight loss
- Reduced cholesterol and improved **cardiovascular (heart) health**

Since many mental health issues are related to stress and lack of sleep, seeing improvements in those areas is a big win. This is true even if you don't have mental health disorders and are just feeling stressed out in general.

When I was working in an office, I loved my lunch time walks, because it was an opportunity to get outside in the fresh air, and away from the stressful office environment. Walking is a great way to take a break if you are working on something difficult and need to step away for a bit.

How much do you need to walk?

You can get these benefits of walking as little as 30 minutes a day. However, if you have been sedentary for a long period of time and are trying to start an exercise routine from scratch, you may want to start smaller.

When I first started going on daily walks, I would just go around the block and then go back to my desk. If you walk so far that you are getting exhausted, that isn't doing you any good. Start off with small, achievable goals. That way, you will be able to increase how far or how long you walk gradually over time.

The ideal number of steps for weight loss is 10,000 steps for day. You can track your steps using your cell phone, or with a fitness tracker (Apple Watch, Fitbit, etc.). When you get your 10,000-step goal every day, then you will really begin to see results and lost weight.

How can I increase my number of steps?

According to Medical News Today, "People can increase the number of steps they take each day by changing some of their daily movement patterns. Tips for doing this include:

- taking the stairs instead of the elevator
- parking further away from the door at shops, work, or school
- walking to lunch, work, school, or other activities if possible
- taking walking breaks at work instead of sitting in a break room

When I first started tracking my steps, I did the "take the stairs challenge" as part of a fitness program for my job. I worked on the 14th floor of an office building, and by the time I walked up all those stairs, I was exhausted, after that I just took the stairs down for a while, until I had more energy.

You can also practice walking up and down stairs at home if you have them. If you walk up and down a couple of extra times a day, that can be great exercise too and less tiring.

Also, walking on an incline in general will burn more calories than walking on a flat surface.

If you live in a downtown area, you can walk up and down steps of buildings during your walk. I did this when I walked from my office. I found several buildings with a lot of steps and incorporated walking past them, so I could go up or down the steps, every day. It doesn't have to change your route; it just gives you get a few more steps going where you always go.

Also, if you are taking a bus or metro to work or school, you can get off one stop earlier and walk the rest of the way to get more steps.

There are many easier ways to incorporate more walking into your day once you are thinking about it, these are only a few suggestions. You can get creative with it and figure out what works best for you.

How fast should you walk?

Medical News Today suggests that to maximize your weight loss, you should walk "briskly," or at a fast pace. It should be a little bit slower than what you would be going if you were jogging.

When you are first starting out with walking, just walk at a pace that is a bit faster than your usual walk. Imagine if you are in a hurry getting to the bus stop or running a little bit late for an appointment and use that pace.

What has worked for me to create a fast pace while walking is to listen to upbeat music. Then, I walk in time with the music. I usually use a club mix so that I end up walking pretty quickly.

Walking can be social.

You can meet up with some friends a couple of times a week, you can go and walk together and help keep each other motivated. You could walk to a park, or to get a coffee together. It's a bonus if you have kids the same age, and you walk them to the park for a play date. That way you can get the kids out of the house too.

If you don't live in a neighborhood with anyone else that you want to walk with, it could be a way to meet people. Some fitness apps let you join teams to compete and track your steps, so you can get social that way as well. Social apps are also a good way to find hiking or walking trails in your area that you may not have known.

If you are going on walks every day in your neighborhood, you may notice others doing the same. If you see the same three ladies walking every day, that may be a great way to make new friends with some healthy habits.

Walking Outside.

When you go for your daily walks outside, you are getting the additional benefit of being in the sun.

Have you ever noticed that sitting outside in the sun can make you feel relaxed and happy? Sunlight has many health benefits that you will be soaking up too.

Healthline serotonin

- Helping Anxiety and Depression
- Help with Panic Attacks
- Building Strong Bones
- Cancer Prevention
- Healing Skin Conditions
- Helping with Autoimmune Conditions

With all these benefits, slap on your SPF and go on your walk outside today!

Get Rewarded for Walking.

These days, there are many of apps that reward you for walking as well. I started off with an app provided by my insurance company to track my steps. If I get up to a certain amount per day, I can earn a free Apple Watch. They sent me the watch at the beginning of the program to track steps, so now I just have to meet my goal each month or make a payment for the watch.

There are other apps like Achievemint or HealthyWage that pay you to track your activities. If you meet your goals, you can win a prize. The amounts vary, but it is a nice incentive to keep you going when you are not feeling motivated.

Conclusion.

There are many great benefits to adding walking to your daily routine. It is a great easy exercise that you can start with right away, and at no cost. With all these benefits, I hope that you will want to start a new walking program to do something good for yourself today.

Yoga is great exercise.

Starting a daily yoga practice, for as little as 10 minutes a day, can also help increase physical and mental wellness significantly.

As busy moms, we don't always think we have time to do things for ourselves. That is partly the reason I started yoga, since it combines exercise with meditation. Both had been recommended to me as coping strategies for the Post-Partum Anxiety I had been experiencing. I didn't think I had time to do both, so I decided I would try something that combined both exercise and meditation into one practice.

Two and a half years later, I never realized that yoga would become such a focal point of my life. Yoga is more than a type of exercise; it is a lifestyle. I love it, and I love the person that it has helped me become.

Practicing Yoga

Yoga is called a practice because it acknowledges that we aren't perfect.
River, my 4-year-old, likes to do yoga with me in the mornings sometimes. The other day our class had us doing chair pose with a prayer twist and she said it was too hard.

I told her it was ok, and that the teacher had shown a modification of the regular chair pose, and I knew she could do that.

I asked her if she knew why doing yoga was called a practice. She didn't, but you know, she is 4.

I explained that yoga is called a practice because we aren't perfect. We get a little better every day, and eventually we learn to do harder things.

I told her, I can't do the hardest version either or take the bind like our teacher. I usually do the medium version of each pose.

She liked that.

Life is a lot like yoga. We can focus on our breath. Relax into things and improve little by little.

I like to teach my kids that we don't have to strive for perfection. Instead, we can focus on getting a little better every day.

That is what I love about yoga. It meets you where you are, while helping you become more connected with yourself, and more accepting of who you are. As someone who struggles with self-acceptance, this has been important for me.

You can do yoga with kids.

Health Benefits of Yoga

According to Johns Hopkins University, (9 Benefits of Yoga | Johns Hopkins Medicine), some of the benefits of yoga include:

1. Improved Strength, balance, and flexibility
2. Back pain relief
3. Eases arthritis symptoms
4. Benefits heart health
5. Relaxes you to help with sleep
6. Contributes to more energy and better moods
7. Helps to manage stress
8. Connects you with a supportive community
9. Leads to better self-care

These benefits can be found even if you are a beginner with yoga and can help people of all ages. You don't have to do the hardest poses to get the greatest benefits. Yoga helps you focus on your breath, be present in the moment, and find mental stillness.

Emotional Benefits of Yoga.

Learning yoga has helped me learn to be gentle with myself, and to listen to my body. Every day our body has different needs. Some days, I want a fast, cardio practice. Other days, I want a slow gentle stretch. I have learned to accept that it isn't sustainable to push my body to its limits every day. Sometimes I need to slow down and rest.

There are videos and tutorials for all different styles of yoga, and quizzes on what yoga style may benefit you at a given time. Since I mainly started yoga because of stress, I usually try to do a very gentle practice if I am feeling tired or unmotivated.

Yin style Yoga provides deep, slow stretches to help release tight and sore muscles. It can also help you relax your mind as you focus on your body and your breath.

There is even yoga just for your face, to help you release your facial muscles. This can help with reducing stress also.

By teaching us physical balance, yoga also teaches us mental balance. It helps connect our mind to our body through our breathing. There are many balancing poses where you stand on one leg, but that isn't the only aspect of balance. When doing our yoga practice, we keep in balance by repeating each pose for each side of our body. This helps create whole-body balance.

Yoga has also helped me to learn the value of self-acceptance. I think that is something that many of us, as moms struggle with. We always place our kids and family first (not that it's a bad thing!), but we neglect ourselves in the process. Mom is a part of the family too, and we are deserving of the same care we provide our children.

When we accept ourselves, it is first accepting that we are important and deserve to honor our needs. It is also about accepting where we are in life, with our physical and mental health. We may not be where we want to be in life, but we can still accept that where we are is ok. We can honor our needs in any given moment.

Accepting where we are, accepting ourselves as we are, doesn't mean we give up on our goals. It means that we accept that our goals will take work. And we are still valuable people while we are on the journey to where we want to be. Meeting goals isn't always linear. We can enjoy the process of self-development, without putting ourselves down for not being perfect.

Often, when we work on health and fitness goals, it can be easy to bash ourselves for being fat, out of shape, tired, eating chocolate, etc. It is important to do things incrementally and not to be too hard on ourselves. Accept that we are work in progress. We aren't going to lose 30 pounds by tomorrow in any type of sustainable way.

When I started Yoga, I did 10 minutes a day for months. Then I started doing 15 minutes. Every time I got comfortable with my practice, I would add more time or more difficulty.

But slowly.

Learning to move slowly and gradually really helped me to reduce my stress level overall.

Spiritual Benefits of Yoga

Yoga began as a part of Hinduism and was a practice that was done by the Hindu priest caste. According to Yoga Basics, "The beginnings of Yoga were developed by the Indus-Sarasvati civilization in Northern India over 5,000 years ago. The word yoga was first mentioned in the oldest sacred texts, the Rig Veda. The Vedas were a collection of texts containing songs, mantras and rituals to be used by Brahmans, the Vedic priests."

Since Yoga was originally practiced by priests, it does have a spiritual element to the practice. I have experienced this in my own life as I learn to bring my mind and body into alignment through practiced breathing. By focusing on the body and the breath, it allows my mind to relax. Instead of thinking about what I need to do all day, or the past and the future, it allows me to focus on my body and to be present.

Being present in my body, and feeling my muscles relax into long-held poses in Yin Yoga, I also feel my mind begin to relax. At the end of one yoga practice recently, I was in my Savasana, and visualizing light entering my body. I felt this overwhelming feeling of peace, light and love.

It is hard to put into words, but it felt like a coming home. It was a feeling of remembrance of our true nature, that of boundless love. We are all a part of one world, one humanity, and we all can have love and compassion for one another. I felt united with that boundless love and it brought me a true peace that I have been seeking. This is how worked for me in any case, while you may have a different experience or none at all, it certainly will give you a slew of exercises that make you healthier.

The Himilayan Yoga Institute describes it like this, "A good yoga practice is one that allows its practitioners to achieve peace – with themselves and the external world they inhabit. The spiritual aspect of yoga emphasizes the attainment of peace and clarity of mind, while perfecting the posture is of secondary importance.

When we practice yoga with a spiritual outlook, we acknowledge that the end purpose is transformation and awakening of our true Inner Self. Awakening of Self means realizing our highest potential. Realizing our hidden potential allows us to express the fullness of our divine essence and to thereby make the greatest possible contribution to the world.

Practicing yoga with this ultimate objective will eventually lead to spiritual fulfillment, a state of great bliss. The practice of yoga aimed at total integration includes a certain lifestyle, the practice of compassion and kindness, a vegetarian or vegan diet, and all of this plays an important role in the fulfillment of the above objective."

With Yoga, you can make a whole new lifestyle, as explained above. Although I originally started doing yoga to decrease my anxiety, as I have delved more deeply into my yoga practice, I have also returned to a more spiritual and mindful lifestyle.

Yoga doesn't have to be spiritual if you don't choose that for yourself. Although Yoga started with religious communities, it is not formally linked to any organized religion today. Yoga itself is not a religion either. You get out of your practice what you choose.

According to Best In Yoga, "Yoga is a way to cultivate wholeness. It can help you remember wholeness and recognize it everywhere. For some yogis, wholeness is the spiritual practice of yoga.

Spirituality helps you trust in life and yourself even when managing difficult situations. When you are connected in the self, inner peace grows. You will find you are more capable of caring and loving for yourself and others and you will experience the joy of being who you are by deepening your yoga practice."

The description of wholeness, is what I described as my experience of oneness. First, you come into oneness with yourself. You can align your body, mind, and spirit through the breath. Then, you may experience a greater oneness as well.

"I am that, you are that, all this is that."

This is an ancient saying, about honoring the divine in everyone. It sort of explains the experience of oneness. Here Deepak Chopra addresses it, "To get at the answer [what is *that*], there's another ancient teaching related to "I Am That," which declares, "This isn't knowledge you learn, it is knowledge you become." In other words, "That" transforms the person having the experience. Being centered is an everyday experience accessible to anyone. The trick is to let the value of the experience sink in deeply, and then a shift begins. You start shedding the burden of effort and struggle. You begin to see that at its source, silent awareness contains infinite resourcefulness, intelligence, creativity, and love."

Oneness, love and peace are a beautiful experience. I always thought I would have to go to a mountain top somewhere to find it. But to my surprise, it was always waiting here for me to find inside my own home.

Different styles of Yoga.

There are many different types of yoga out there and choosing which type of yoga is right for you will likely depend on why you are wanting to start a yoga practice.

Do you want to do yoga for exercise? Are you interested in reducing anxiety symptoms? Do you want a better balance?

These are just a few of the reasons that women just like us have started doing yoga. Here are all the types of yoga, and what they can help with. According to Yoga Medicine, here are the different types of yoga.

- **Kundalini Yoga** - Is good for "Anyone in search of a physical, yet also spiritual practice, or those who like singing or chanting." This type of practice works by "challenging both mind and body with chanting, singing, meditation, and *kriyas* (specific series of poses paired with breath work and chanting). You might notice everyone is wearing white, as it's believed to deflect negativity and increase your aura. Typically, a kundalini class starts with a mantra (a focus for the class), then includes breathing exercises, warmups to get the body moving, increasingly more challenging poses, and a final relaxation and meditation."
- **Vinyasa Yoga** - This is one of the most common styles of yoga, that goes through a routine called a flow. "Vinyasa flow is a style of yoga where the poses are synchronized with the breath in a continuous rhythmic flow," says Sherrell Moore-Tucker, RYT 200. "The flow can be meditative in nature, calming the mind and nervous system, even though you're moving." This style of yoga is great for anyone who prefers movement to stillness throughout their yoga practice.
- **Hatha Yoga** - This is a style of yoga focused on creating balance. "The balance in hatha yoga might come from strength and flexibility, physical and mental energy, or breath and the body." Hatha yoga is slower moving, and focused on breath, which makes it a great style for anyone looking for a more gentle type of practice.
- **Ashtanga Yoga** - This style of yoga is great for anyone who likes a routine, which is mostly physical and yet spiritual too. "Ashtanga yoga consists of six series of specific poses taught in order. Each pose and each series is "given" to a student when their teacher decides they have mastered the previous one. This is a very physical, flow-style yoga with spiritual components"
- **Yin Yoga** - This style of yoga is slower, with participants holding their poses for 2 minutes or more. It can be used to stretch out after doing other exercise, or by anyone looking for a slower type

of practice. Also, "While other forms of yoga focus on the major muscle groups, yin yoga targets the body's connective tissues."

- **Iyengar Yoga** - This type of yoga is good for anyone who wants a more static yoga practice, which is good for any type of physical limitations. "While considered optional in many practices, multiple props are used in Iyengar classes — including chairs, walls, and benches, in addition to more common ones like straps, blocks, and bolsters."
- **Bikram Yoga** - A form of hot yoga, "These classes, like ashtanga classes, consist of a set series of poses performed in the same order, and the practice has strict rules. Each class is 90 minutes, with 26 postures and two breathing exercises, and the room must be 105° Fahrenheit with 40 percent humidity." The purpose of hot yoga is to allow for greater sweat and flexibility.
- **Power Yoga** - Power yoga is a more fast-paced yoga practice with less of a spiritual component. According to practitioners, "power yoga strengthens the muscles while also increasing flexibility. The variation of sequences keeps the brain engaged while you work all muscle groups in the body."
- **Prenatal Yoga** - Prenatal yoga is a great way for expectant mothers to work out in a gentle way. "Since this is a practice designed specifically for moms-to-be, it excludes poses that might be too taxing or unsafe for the changing body."

Which style of yoga you choose may vary depending on what type of benefits you are looking to get. Yoga has many benefits for your physical, mental, and spiritual health.

You may even choose different styles of yoga on different days once you get a sense of what your body needs. Personally, I tend to alternate between Vinyasa or Power Yoga for exercise, and Yin Yoga for mental clarity or to release stress. Our needs from one day to the next may not be the same, so it is great to try different styles of yoga to meet different needs.

Getting Started as a Beginner

When I started doing yoga, I was a busy mom with a baby that didn't sleep through the night. I was physically and mentally exhausted, and not losing the baby weight either. I had heard from some girls that I worked with that yoga was a great easy exercise and even would help with my postpartum anxiety.

I didn't think I had time in my schedule to sign up for an hour-long class at a gym, so I started off with easy videos on YouTube that I could do at home. All I had to buy was a yoga mat.

There are tons of great yoga videos out there, and tutorials on how to do different poses.

When I first started doing yoga, I searched for the shortest beginner videos that I could find. I found a whole playlist with 10-minute easy beginner videos. That really helped make Yoga accessible to me as a beginner.

Conclusion.

Whether you want to improve your physical, mental, or spiritual well-being, yoga is a great way to do that.

Since I have started doing yoga, I have gained strength and flexibility. I can get up from sitting on the ground with my toddler. I can lift things that are heavier, because of the bodyweight exercises. I have toned my arms, legs, and abs.

Yoga also helps me to cope with my anxiety better than anything else has. I remember when I felt anxious that I could return to my breath. A deep, slow breath at any time can be calming. As yoga calms my mind, I can remember that calm throughout the day by connecting with my breath.

Finally, yoga has helped me feel a return to spirituality. I can connect to a deep peacefulness that I find during yoga at any time that I need it. Once you find peace, you realize that peace is always there.

You can experience these benefits, and many others by starting a yoga practice.

10

Mental Health

Good mental health is essential to our overall health. According to MentalHealth.gov, "Mental health includes our emotional, psychological, and social well-being. It affects how we think, feel, and act. It also helps determine how we handle stress, relate to others, and make choices. Mental health is important at every stage of life, from childhood and adolescence through adulthood."

Typically, we think of mental health only in terms of mental illness, but mental health is an important aspect of health for all of us. Stress can greatly impact our mental health, and there are many ways that we can take care of ourselves to keep from getting to the point where toxic stress severely impacts our mental health.

Get control of your finances.

I know getting control of your finances doesn't really sound like a mental health issue, but it can be, since money is a huge cause of stress. According to CNBC, "73% of Americans rank their finances as their No. 1 stress in life." Since our financial health is a leading cause of stress, getting your finances under control can mean a big reduction in your stress level and consequently improve your health and happiness as well.

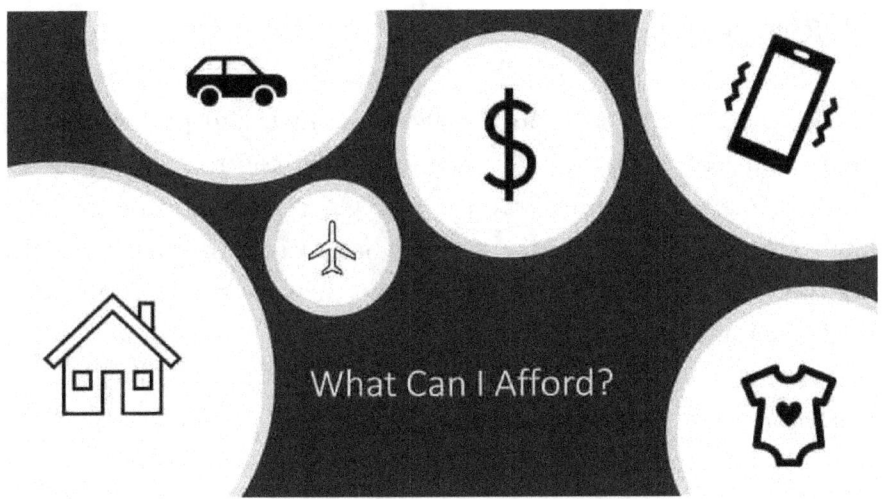

What Can I Afford?

Are You Stressed about money?

Do you ask yourself questions for instance:

- Why do I never have any money?
- How am I going to make it until payday?
- How can I get some money fast?
- What frugal living habits can I adopt?
- Why are all my credit card payments going to interest?
- How am I ever going to pay all this debt?
- How am I going to pay for my childcare this month?
- Am I going to lose my house?
- Can bill collectors garnish my wages?

After learning some personal finance basics to implement in your life, you will be able to start getting your finances on track, starting today. Since money can be a big cause of stress, this is very important.

Making a Budget

Making a budget for your family is the first, and probably most important, step to getting your finances under control. So, if you are anything like me, go look through that giant stack of papers in the kitchen for your bills. It may take a while to sort through the kid's drawings and Chinese food menus to find them, but you are going to thank me for it later.

Keeping track of your bills, your income, and your spending will set a baseline for your finances. There are many ways to set up a budget, from using a notebook and writing them down old-school, to apps that automatically sync with your bank account.

Since I have spent years working with budgets, I typically have gone with MS Excel for my budget spreadsheet in the past. The last couple years though, I have migrated into Google Sheets, because of the ease of accessing my budget from anywhere. Another difference between MS Excel and Google Sheets is that Google Sheets is free, whereas Microsoft requires a paid subscription or download of their software. Most of the basic functionalities of the two programs is the same, I find I only need the advanced functionality in Excel for typing spreadsheets that need to use VLOOKUP's. (If you don't know what that is, not to worry, it probably means that you don't need it)

Whatever format you choose for your budget, the basics remain the same. You will want to have a section for your income, and another section for your bills. Then, a comparison of the two to determine if you have a positive or negative cash flow. (we will discuss more about cash flow later)

Personally, I also like to have columns for the amount due, date due, and date paid. Some people are OK with having a simplified form that just tracks the amounts you have actually paid. The benefit of having the additional column is so that you will be able to track, for example, if you have paid an additional amount on a credit card or your mortgage payment in order to pay your bills down faster.

Here is an example of what your budget spreadsheet may look like.

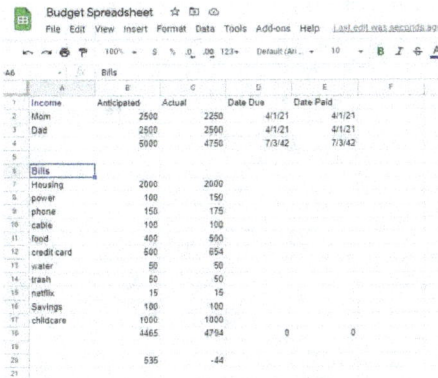

The spreadsheet shows:

	A	Anticipated	Actual	Date Due	Date Paid	F
1	Income	Anticipated	Actual	Date Due	Date Paid	
2	Mom	2500	2250	4/1/21	4/1/21	
3	Dad	2500	2500	4/1/21	4/1/21	
4		5000	4750	7/3/42	7/3/42	
5						
6	Bills					
7	Housing	2000	2000			
8	power	100	190			
9	phone	150	175			
10	cable	100	100			
11	food	400	500			
12	credit card	500	654			
13	water	50	50			
14	trash	50	50			
15	netflix	15	15			
16	Savings	100	100			
17	childcare	1000	1000			
18		4465	4794	0	0	
19						
20		535	-44			
21						

Make Your Own Budget

Income	Anticipated Amount	Actual Amount	Date	
In Savings				
Payroll				
Other Income				
Total	0	0		

Expenses	Minimum Payment	Actual Payment	Date Due	Date Paid
Mortgage				
Water				
Sewer				
Trash				
Electric				
Savings				
Credit Card				
Student Loans				

Total	0	0		
Remaining Balance	0	0		

Understand Your Financial Situation.

Once you have made a budget, you will be able to see where all your hard-earned cash is going. It's important to know if you are in a positive cash flow (where your income is more than your bills), or a negative cash flow (where your bills are more than your income). Once you know where you stand, then you can start taking control over your money.

Look at "Problem Areas" In Your Budget.

Once you have made a budget, and looked to see if anything is in collections, look at everything you are spending money on that isn't a bill.

Do you have a lot of car repairs? Large phone bill? Do so much online shopping you forget what you ordered until it shows up at your door?

Whatever the case may be, look at how you are handling your problem spending areas. Are they things you were already aware of? Or did they catch you by surprise?

Often, we spend money on a day-to-day basis on "small" things that really add up in the end. Recently, my partner noticed that he was buying Gatorades at the gas station for $3 each. At the supermarket, they are 4 for $5. So, he started buying them at home to take with him in the morning. I know saving $2 per day doesn't seem like much until you figure that this single item adds up to at least $40 a month. But if there are multiple items like this that you are buying for a more expensive price due to convenience, it is easy to rethink *where* you buy things.

Frugal hacks like this can easily be incorporated into your daily life. You can buy some items at the dollar store or other discount stores more cheaply than at the supermarket. Or you can look at weekly ad flyers from each local store to ensure that you are getting the best price.

Either way, now that you are truly aware of problem spending areas, it is time to talk to your spouse about your financial hardships and plan together on how to tackle them. It is important for couples to work as a team on finances, as that is one of the top things that couples typically argue about.

When you and your spouse or significant other can work as a team to confront a problem, then it is the two of you against the problem, instead of the two of you against each other. That is so important about making your relationship work.

Next Steps for a Positive Cash Flow.

If your budget is in a positive cash flow where you have money left over after you pay your bills, that may mean you are spending more money than necessary on items that are not in your budget.

The first thing to look at in this case would be your online banking screen. Look at all the transactions that are not bills and write them down by category.

Do you spend money on eating out? Subscription boxes? Coffee? Toys for the kiddos? Lunch at work? All of these things are easy to work on reevaluating one by one if they are eating up a lot of money.

What if my bills place me in a negative cash flow?

If you are in a negative cash flow, there are many things that you can do to take control of your financial situation. Sometimes there are bills that you can negotiate a price or shop around. This would be like your phone bill, insurance, or trash service. It does take time to shop around for a cheaper price, but with many of these it is a good idea to shop around every 6 months.

If your bills are mostly credit cards, which was the case for me, you can try to call the credit card companies one at a time, and ask if they have any type of plan to either skip a payment or to lower your interest rate. Again, it may help to do this every few months to see if new programs become available.

Once you have tried these options and you are still struggling, it may be time to consider credit card consolidation, or filing for a bankruptcy. While Bankruptcy is in my opinion a plan of last resort, in some cases, such as, a large pile of medical bills or after a long-term disability, it may very well become the only solution to getting you back on track.

When I was a kid, my parents had to declare bankruptcy twice, so they weren't really the best example for me of what responsible spending looks like. You may have had an upbringing like mine, with a lack of responsible role models to teach you about your finances.

I think that is true for many of us, and we must learn the hard way when our own bills go into collections.

Hopefully, you are not in this category, but right now with the way the economy is, I wouldn't be surprised. There are so many of us who lost our jobs, or lost hours in the last year, it is unprecedented in our lifetimes.

For us Millennials that grew up in the Clinton Era and afterward, we had no idea that a depression like this could come in our lifetimes. We thought, if we work hard and pay our bills on time, then everything would be fine.

Do you have bills in collections?

If that is the case, this is what you will probably want to work on paying off first, as it can have a drastic negative impact on your credit. Typically, if you have bills in collections, you will receive some angry letters in the mail. Once you do get collection letters in the mail, you have several ways to deal with collection agencies. Partly, this will depend on the amounts that you owe and on what your short-term financial goals are. Before we tackle what to do, you will also want to check your credit report to determine if there are any other outstanding bills you aren't aware of.

Checking Your Credit Score

After making a budget, the next thing you need to know when it comes to your finances is how to check your credit score.

Your credit can affect your ability to make major purchases such as a house or a car. It also determines if you will qualify for a credit card or a loan. Some employers even check your credit score when you apply for a job, while it sounds crazy, it may show an employer how responsible/reliable you are or if your personal life will cause possible problems for the company later.

Since credit impacts so many other areas of your finances, it is important to be aware of what is on your credit report, and to know your credit score.

There are three main credit bureaus:

- Experian
- Equifax
- Transunion

Each one determines your credit score in a slightly different way. When you apply for most credit products, they will usually take an average of your credit scores from all three bureaus.

Credit Report Vs. Credit Score

Your credit report is a list of all of your creditors that report to the credit bureau. It will include any credit cards, loans, and any collections. A collection is a bill that has been reported as being unpaid.

Using your credit report, the credit bureau will determine your credit score. They use a formula that combines the following factors:

- Amount of Outstanding Debt
- On Time vs. Late Payments
- Credit Utilization
- Age of Accounts
- Amount of Credit Inquiries

Different bureaus will weight each factor slightly differently. But all of them will reduce your credit score the most based on late payments and collections.

How do I get my Credit Report & Score?

If you have a major credit card, there is probably a section of your app that will tell you your credit score. It may also be on your statement. Make sure that if it does tell you a credit score, that you look to see if it is your FICO score. This is the score that mortgage lenders use. There are other types of scores, but they are not very useful. If you go to a mortgage lender and give them another type of score, it can be very misleading, and you may not end up qualifying for a loan when you thought you would.

If your credit card doesn't show your FICO score, don't worry!

To get the official 3-bureau credit report, you can go to www.annualcreditreport.com and request it. Everyone is allowed to request a copy of their credit report once a year. You are also allowed to request your credit report if you have other things happen, like being denied credit. The only problem is that the free credit report doesn't give your credit score. They make you pay for it.

However, you can check your credit score for free on several different websites. But again, be wary, as some of these are not very accurate. In my experience, the score that you get from www.creditkarma.com is going to be the closest to your FICO score. They also will give you tips on raising your score, although many of these will involve applying for new credit cards. I would advise not applying unless you want a new credit card.

I have my Credit Report, now what?

Once you have a copy of your report, verify everything is correct. In other words, make sure all the bills on there are bills that you currently have.

If there is anything on the report that you don't recognize, this may mean you have been a victim of identity theft. If this is the case, you will want to call your bank right away to notify them.

After that, you will need to dispute the items on your credit report that are in error. To do this, you will need to go to each credit bureau website and follow their directions for disputing an item on the credit report. You will usually receive a response in about 30 days. If they don't remove the item from your credit report, you may need to provide additional information.

Once you have done this, you will be well on your way to having your financial future in hand.

What if my credit score is bad?

If your credit is bad, then you will want to determine the reason for this. If it is due to identity theft, that is self-explanatory, and should sort itself out once you dispute the fraudulent items.

There are several other reasons you could have a low credit score, and Credit Karma is useful for determining that as well. If it is because of late payments, then make sure you start to make payments on time. You need to have about a years' worth of on time payments to bring up your score.

If it is because of collections, then you will probably want to dispute those on your credit report as well. Or you can work with the collection agencies to settle them from your report.

There are only two other reasons your credit score would be low. First is if you have little to no credit history. That is not a bad place to be in, it just means that you need to build up your credit.

The other reason is if you have high credit utilization, that means, most of your credit cards are probably maxed out. There are a couple of things you can do in this case. First, you can just make your normal payments and wait for your score to go up as your credit balance goes down.

Or, if you are in a bit of a hurry, you can apply for a credit limit increase on your cards. You would still owe the same amount, but you have more available credit. That will make your score go up. The only problem with this method is that, depending on your score in the first place, you might not qualify.

Do you have bills in collections?

If so, this is what you will probably want to work on paying off first, as it can have a drastic negative impact on your credit. Typically, if you have bills in collections, you will receive some angry letters in the mail. Once you do get collection letters in the mail, you have several ways to deal with collection agencies. Partly, this will depend on the amounts that you owe, how much money you have and on what your short-term financial goals are.

Once you get into a lot of debt that you cannot pay easily, it can become very stressful and seem like an insurmountable task at times. I was in that position when I got divorced, and I used several different strategies to deal with collections. If you think you may have the ability to slowly pay your collections monthly, you can try to negotiate with the collection agencies yourself. Otherwise, you can hire several different types of companies to help you work with the collection agencies instead.

Something noteworthy about collection agencies is to know that they have bought your debt from the original creditor for pennies on the dollar, that leaves some room for negotiation. Keep in mind if you don't pay the collection agency, they will sell your debt to a different collection agency. Every time that happens, you get another negative mark onto your credit report. That means, the longer that you go without paying a bill that is in collections, the worse your credit will get.

Ask Family for a Loan.

If you are on good terms with your extended family, this can be a good first step. If for example, you have $3,000 in credit card bills, and they are charging you 20% interest (a typical credit card rate), then you are paying a good portion of your monthly bill towards interest, instead of paying down the principal. If you are able to get a loan from your family, you could pay the same amount each month and pay the debt off faster.

When you go to talk to your family, it is a good idea to take a copy of your monthly budget, as well as your credit report. That way, you can show them everything that you are paying, and how much of it is interest. You should also be able to present them with a proposed repayment plan. That way, they will know that you are serious about paying them back.

Talking to your family about your finances can sometimes be difficult and stressful, but it can help you get out of a large amount of debt much more quickly. If your family has extra money, they may also be willing to give you a month or two without a payment so that you are able to get back on your feet a little bit before you begin making payments.

Once you come to an agreement, it is important to stick to it. Money is one of the main things that people will argue about, it is important to keep your word on your payment plan, and you will keep in good relations with your family.

If for some reason they are unable to loan you the money, it is also important not to take it personally or hold a grudge. They may be struggling financially as well, and currently unable to assist you. If this is the case, you can talk to them about the possibility of getting a loan at a later time instead, once they are in a better position to help you.

Get A Personal Loan.

For some of us, getting a loan from family is not possible for a variety of reasons. If this is the case for you, then you may want to consider getting a personal loan instead. There are a variety of companies that offer personal loans even if your credit isn't great. These will typically be at a lower interest rate than what you are paying for your credit card payments.

First, it can be a good idea to talk to your bank or financial institution. Many will offer personal loans for their current customers. This will typically be the lowest interest rate that you will find. If you can go through your bank to get a loan to consolidate your credit cards, this will put you in a much better position. You will then only have one monthly payment instead of several, and it will be less interest and typically a lower monthly payment. Some banks will offer an additional discount on the interest rate if you can set up the payments through direct deposit.

If your bank doesn't offer personal loans or you don't qualify, there are many other companies where you can get a personal loan. We talked previously about logging into Credit Karma to check your credit score, and this is also a good place to look for a personal loan.

If you look at the top of the dashboard in Credit Karma, there is a menu for loans.

Personal loans

Tell us what you're looking for.

How much are you looking to borrow?

$10,000

What's your credit score?

Excellent (750 - 850) ∨

Search

Loan offers tailored to you

Log in or sign up to see offers that are personalized to your financial profile.

You will be able to type in some information about your situation, and then you will get a list of loan offers. Then, you will be able to compare the loan term (how long you have to pay back the loan) as well as the interest rates and payments. Once you find the best loan product, you will be able to click on a link to apply online. Many online loans will allow you to apply and receive your funds the same day or the next day.

In the past I have gotten loans through both Upstart and Marcus. I was happy with both of them, and both offer lower rates if you have automatic payments set up. Another good feature is that they don't have a prepayment penalty. That means, you can pay the loan off sooner if you get some extra money. This may not always be the case with a bank loan.

Get a Balance Transfer Card.

If you have good credit but high interest or payments, you may also qualify for a 0% interest credit card, that you can use to transfer the balance from a higher interest card or cards. You can use Credit Karma to search for these as well, or you can look for offers from your current credit card company.

Typically, cards that offer a 0% interest on balance transfers will only do so for a certain length of time. It will usually be for 12-18 months.

So, it is important to keep in mind that if you can't pay off the balance in that time, the card will start charging the higher interest rate again.

Sometimes, you will be able to transfer the remaining amount to another 0% interest card 2 or 3 times before you stop qualifying for another credit card. This is a temporary fix, but not always the best option if you owe a lot in credit cards. The best way is to pay off the entire amount before the 0% rate expires.

Negotiate with the Collection Agencies

When I got divorced, I wasn't aware of any type of help that was available to deal with collection agencies, so I negotiated with all creditors myself. It can be an incredibly stressful and time-consuming process, but it will get the calls to stop.

To negotiate with collection agencies, you can look at all the letters that they send in the mail to see how much you owe. Then you can either call them or wait for them to call you. When you speak with them, have in mind an amount that you can pay per month. You can offer them as little as $50 per month, to show them that you are willing to pay something. Sometimes, they will have a set amount that they allow you to pay, and it will be more than you anticipate.

For example, if you offer $50, and they want you to pay $100, you can agree or offer something like $75 or you can hold firm at the original $50. Let them know that it is all that you can afford, and they either get the $50 or they get nothing. If they won't make a deal that is reasonable, then you can simply not pay them and wait until you get a better offer.

Sometimes, if you owe quite a lot of money, or if something has been in collections for a long time, a collection agency will settle with you for less than what you owe. Sometimes, it will be as little as half of the original amount. If you really want to play hard-ball and pay as little as possible, you can wait for this type of offers. Collection agencies are most often willing to settle for less if you can pay the whole payment at once.

When paying off collections, there are several routes that you can go. You can pay a little on each bill at the same time, you can start with the smallest amount first, or you can start with the bill that gives you the best offer. Whatever method that you choose, it can take a while to pay them all off.

Once you have paid off all the collections, you may want to investigate Credit Counseling (in a later chapter) to get all of the paid collections removed from your credit report. This can be helpful because even paid collections can hurt your credit report. You can also make it part of your negotiations with the collection agency and let them know that you are only willing to pay the debt if it is removed from your credit report. Not all of them will be willing to do so, but the more you can get removed this way, the better your credit will be in the long run.

Otherwise, if you have more time before needing to make a major purchase or get new credit, you can wait for the collections to fall off your credit report. After 7 years, old collections roll off your credit report.

Debt Consolidation

Debt consolidation is like what I described in the previous section about negotiating with creditors to get all your collections paid off. The main difference is that you are hiring a company to work with the creditors on your behalf, instead of doing everything yourself. This can be less stressful, as all you do is make a payment to a trust account each month, until everything is paid off and tell creditors to call the consolidation company.

According to Nerd Wallet, "Debt consolidation rolls multiple debts, typically high-interest debt such as credit card bills, into a single payment. Debt consolidation might be a good idea for you if you can get a lower interest rate. That will help you reduce your total debt and reorganize it so you can pay it off faster." Meaning, you can use debt consolidation prior to bills going into collections, to pay the bills off faster.

There are less qualifications for debt consolidation than there are for bankruptcy, which is regulated by many laws. This may be a better option if you are able to pay your bills at all. According to Nerd Wallet, "Debt management plans roll several debts into one monthly payment at a reduced interest rate. It works best for those who are struggling to pay off credit card debt but don't qualify for other options because of a low credit score.

Unlike some credit card consolidation options, debt management plans don't affect your credit score. If your debt is more than 40% of your income and can't be repaid within five years, then bankruptcy may be a better option.

You can find a debt management plan through a nonprofit credit counseling agency."

Credit Counseling

Credit counseling can help you to get derogatory marks removed from your credit report. In some instances, they will do this by advising you on what to pay off, in other instances they will dispute items on your credit report. The different services available may depend on if you have already paid off all your collections already, or you still have more outstanding.

Personally, I used a credit counseling service a couple of years after I paid off all my collections. I was getting ready to buy a house, and I needed to clean up my credit report. The credit counseling company was able to remove the bulk of the paid collections off my credit report, so that I had a good enough credit score to buy my house.

There are non-profit credit counseling services, or for-profit companies. Prior to hiring one, it is good to check their reviews on the Better Business Bureau, to make sure that it is a reputable company. You will want to be sure that the company you choose has a good rating, so that you aren't putting your finances into the hands of someone disreputable. By experience I found that a company charging a flat fee instead of month to month was better.

The Better Business Bureau (BBB) is a non-profit website that you can look at to see if a company has any complaints filed against them by their customers. This will let you know if a company is reputable to do business with. The BBB rates all types of companies, but it is especially important to check with regard to any financial services provider. It is one thing if a restaurant burns your food, but you want a financial company that is not going to lose all your money or scam you.

According to Nerd Wallet, "The National Foundation for Credit Counseling is the nation's largest nonprofit financial counseling organization. It offers a localized search tool that can help you find an affiliated agency nearby with specialists who are right for your financial situation. You also can call 800-388-2227 to be automatically connected to the NFCC member agency closest to you.

The U.S. Department of Justice has its own search tool to help consumers find a credit counseling agency. This list is limited to agencies that provide bankruptcy counseling, but many provide other services as well, and all are vetted by the federal government."

You can look up either of these resources to find credit counseling services, or you can google agencies that work in your area. The company I went with was a for-profit company and worked well for me. So, don't rule it out if you want a non-profit. Really, what it comes down to is looking at all the reviews to be sure you are working with a good company.

Filing Bankruptcy

Filing bankruptcy will have to be the last option that you use to get rid of collections, as in most states they require you to try another option, such as debt consolidation, prior to being able to file.

There are different types of bankruptcy, it will depend what type of bills that you have, and if you have a house or a car that you are wanting to keep.

You can file a bankruptcy on your own if you are able to understand the regulations. However, before you do file, they will require you to attend several classes to understand the process. This can save you some more money than hiring an attorney.

Otherwise, you can hire a bankruptcy attorney to help you navigate the process. Some will offer you a free consultation to talk through your options. It may be a good idea to go to this type of consultation with an attorney (or several) prior to filing, even if you don't ultimately hire them. Typically, attorneys will specialize in bankruptcy, and be able to guide you through the process.

Since the process will be slightly different depending on what state you live in, it is good to look up the bankruptcy laws for your state to see if you will qualify. If not, it may be best to consider credit counseling or debt consolidation instead.

Apply for Social Programs.

If something has happened to you suddenly that negatively impacts your financial situation, in addition to the other strategies listed above you may want to apply for State programs like Medicaid, TANF or Food Stamps. This will get you some short-term assistance if, for instance, you have lost your job or had your hours cut back.

Usually, you will need to go to a city or county office to apply for any or all these programs. Here in Colorado you can fill out an online application for all of the programs that you qualify for at the same time. Colorado also has childcare assistance, so that you will be able to keep your child in daycare if you are looking for a new job or are below a certain income threshold.

Additionally, some county offices will have a Workforce Center, where you can get assistance with finding a job, updating your resume, or learning new job skills. Some will also offer job fairs at their location to make finding a new job easier.

Medicaid is a government program that provides health insurance to people with a low income. You can apply for this even if you are currently working.

TANF is Temporary Assistance for Needy Families. This is a cash assistance program that will help you for a few months if you have lost your job.

Food Stamps are like a little credit card that you get just to pay for groceries. You can get this if you are working or unemployed. They will help you for up to a year if you make below a certain income amount.

Childcare Assistance is available to families that are under a certain income level, to assist with the cost of paying for daycare for small children.

Energy Assistance is also available to help pay the cost of your heating or cooling bill, so that you aren't crushed under the weight of paying yet another bill. This program may also help to winterize your home so that you aren't using so much energy for heating.

All these programs may take a while to apply for, but it is well worth it if you are struggling financially. You will also get a caseworker who can work with you one on one to understand your family's situation and your needs. The caseworker may be able to refer you to additional local services as well. For example, I was referred to my therapist by the TANF office when I had lost my job because of PTSD and panic attacks. (I also wrote a book on panic attacks if you need help in that area)

Community programs can work in combination with any of the other strategies, so that you will have some temporary financial help while you work on a plan to get your finances on track long term.

Setting Financial Goals

When thinking about your budget, collections, or what else you want to do with your money, it will depend on what your financial goals are. You can use some of the additional goal planning worksheets at the end of this book to write about your financial goals as you are going through this section.

Financial trouble typically can be solved in either of two ways: lowering your bills or making more money. Typically, it is easier to lower your bills than it is to increase your income. However, nothing is stopping you from trying both.

Before you decide, think about your short-term and long-term goals for your finances. Do you want to:

- Lower your debt and pay off bills?
- Make a big purchase like a house or a car?
- Have children attending college?
- Want to retire soon?

Depending on where you are at in life, your goals may be very different. The way you handle your money and your credit may be very different too. If you are young and single, you may be able to downsize more easily, like with getting roommates, or riding the bus instead of driving. If you have kids, you will have additional associated expenses like daycare, sports and clubs, college, or medical expenses. If you are ready for retirement, you may also be looking to downsize, or to sell your home to travel.

No matter what your goals are, there are strategies that you can use to meet them. But first, it is important to know what your goals are, and to write them out. If you have a partner, it is best to talk about your financial goals together to decide on a sound plan that you can work on together.

If you are looking at either investments or retirement, it may be best to consult with a financial advisor as well. Many large companies will have a meeting once a year to talk about retirement savings plans that they have available, as well as the pros and cons of investing. They may also tell you how much you need to invest monthly to have enough money for a comfortable retirement. If your employer doesn't offer a service like this, you may need to investigate consulting with a private financial advisor. As with the credit counselor or bankruptcy attorney, it is important to look at reviews, and ratings with the Better Business Bureau.

Creating a Savings Plan

Once you have gotten your bills on the way to being paid off successfully, the next important financial step to take is setting up a savings plan.

"Always pay yourself first!"

This is advice that I got years ago from a friend's dad. He told me, it's important to make saving a priority in your life, and to do it first thing at the beginning of the month. Usually, we think of saving money as something that we will do after we have all our other ducks in a row. The problem is, if we wait to have "extra" money, we are never going to start saving.

No matter where you are with your finances, it is always important to put money into savings, "for a rainy day," as the saying goes. Some important advice is to have enough money in your savings account to pay for between 3-6 months' worth of your bills.

According to Vanguard, "Putting aside 3 to 6 months' worth of expenses is a good rule of thumb, but sometimes it's not enough.

If you're able, you might want to think about expanding your emergency savings.

Here are some scenarios where having more in your savings could benefit you:

- During a recession (when unemployment rates are higher, and the length of unemployment is often longer).
- If you're in a high-risk industry where layoffs are common.
- If your income isn't steady.
- If you're retired (and most of your money is in more-volatile stock and bond investments)."

Years ago, my ex-husband and I were both tipped workers. We would come home after work every night and put 10% of the tips into a jar for ourselves, and 10% into a jar for our daughter. Just by doing this, without having a savings account, we saved up enough money to buy a business in *two years.*

That's right ladies, we saved up enough in TWO YEARS to buy our bar.

The trick is, there is no trick. Anyone can do this. Just make sure that your savings is the first thing you put money into. Of course, it is much easier now a days with linked checking and savings accounts, you can just have an automatic transfer set up for each time you get paid. Then place your savings amount into your budget as a bill.

Set it and Forget it.

One of the important things when it comes to saving money, is to be consistent, I cannot stress this enough.

Build your savings into your budget like a bill. Your first, and most important bill.

Whether you do a set amount, or a set percentage, saving will become a habit. Like with anything we do, building good habits when it comes to our money is very important. Even if it is only $5 or $10 a month, getting into the habit of savings will help you in the future. Then, once you get used to saving that much, you can increase a little more at a time.

Many savings accounts these days have the option to set up automatic transfers from your savings account to your checking account. I have mine set up every paycheck to set aside a certain amount by automatically transferring to savings.

There are also many different apps now that allow you to do the same thing. Some will have incentives for saving a certain amount of money or saving for a certain amount of months in a row. This provides a bonus for saving more money.

What Type of Savings Product Should I Choose?

There are many different types of investment products out there and it seems like everyone gives you different advice. IRA? 401K? Life Insurance? Money Market Account? Stocks? Bonds?

There are advantages to each different type of savings plan. In many ways, it depends on what stage you are at in life what type of product will be best.

Things to ask yourself are:

- Do you want the money to be available easily?
- How much do you have to save?
- How long until retirement?
- Is there a big purchase that you are saving for?
- Do you own a house?

The answers to these questions can help to determine what type of plan may be best for you. Remember, any type of interest-bearing account will help you get more money faster. That is the main reason why you would want to put your funds into a savings account instead of stuffing it under the bed like grandma.

Also, you know that old saying, "Don't put all your eggs into one basket." That applies here too. It is good to set up several different savings plans.

Personally, I would say that having a high interest savings account, life insurance, and a retirement account can be good for most people.

High Interest Savings Account

A high interest savings account is just what it sounds like, a savings account with a higher than usual interest rate. These types of accounts may have additional restrictions that allow them to provide a higher interest rate. Some of the restrictions may be requiring a higher amount of money to open the account, or only allowing a certain number of withdrawals per month.

According to Bankrate, currently Marcus and American Express have the top ranked high interest savings accounts. Both allow you to open an account for only $1. Over time, the best savings products do change, so just make sure that you are comparing based on the interest rate, amount of monthly withdrawals, and the amount required to open the account when you are choosing a product.

I would highly recommend opening a high interest savings account as soon as possible, so you can maximize the earnings on your savings. Even if you only deposit a little bit of money each month, the higher interest rate will allow you to save more money more quickly.

Life Insurance

Life insurance is good to have no matter what if you have kids. Also, the younger and healthier you are when you sign up for life insurance, the lower your monthly cost will be. That is because life insurance is always going to pay out eventually, but the company wants to make sure you are paying as long as possible. So, don't wait until you are sick or old to get life insurance. The best time to get it is always now.

In addition to paying costs for your dependents during end-of-life planning, there are types of life insurance that can be used as savings products as well. These are called Universal or Whole Life policies. Whereas a "term" life insurance policy will only be good for a certain amount of time (Usually 10 or 20 years) whole and universal life insurance policies don't expire. They also allow you to build cash values, that can be taken out as a loan, or at retirement.

According to Forbes, "Universal life insurance is a type of permanent life insurance. It can cover you for the duration of your life, if the premiums are paid. Some forms of universal life insurance also offer a cash value component.

The cash value can build up investment gains (and sometimes get hit with losses, depending on the policy type).

You can take money out of cash value via a withdrawal or loan. The insurance company will reduce the payout to your beneficiaries by the amount of any withdrawals or outstanding loans if you pass away. But for some buyers, accessing cash value is more important than a full payout to beneficiaries later on."

Since it builds up a cash value, the monthly payment for a whole or universal life insurance policy will be more expensive than the monthly payment for a term life insurance. So, depending on your long-term and short-term financial goals, you can investigate one of these three types of life insurance.

Retirement Account

There are many different types of retirement accounts, depending on your employer. You may be eligible for a 401K plan through your job, sometimes your employer will even match a certain percentage of your contribution.

If you don't have an employment sponsored plan, you can also investigate an IRA retirement account.

There are also different types of retirement accounts that are specific to government service, or through the military.

Whatever type of account you decide to get, it is a good idea to start your retirement account as soon as possible. That way, you can save up for as long as possible, and you may not need to save as much each month, since these are interest bearing accounts. If you deposit $10 per month for 20 years, you will earn more in interest than you do if you deposit $20 per month for 10 years. That is why it is important to start saving as soon as possible, even if you don't have much to set aside.

Earning More Money

As you are looking at getting your bills under control, you may also want to look into ways that you can earn more money as well. Here are some basic tips to get you started.

Get a promotion at work

Getting a promotion at work may sound easier said than done, and it is rarely something that will happen quickly, unless you are currently underemployed in your field. Then it doesn't require you to look for a new job, go to school, or work a hundred hours per week.

If you like the field that you currently work in, and are satisfied with your job overall, this may be your best bet.

Before you apply for a promotion, you will want to lay the ground-work and show that you are a model employee. To do this, make sure that you are always on time for work, find coverage if you call in sick, and that you are not seen as being a complainer. It is also good to show that you are a go-getter by presenting useful ideas on how to improve operations, just be sure that you always present them in a constructive and helpful manner.

Trying to get a promotion will take time, it also takes showing a growing expertise in your field. You can grow your skills every day and gradually take on new and more difficult tasks. It also is good to keep current in your field by reading journals, news or linked in articles to keep abreast of new advances in your field. This shows that you are committed to your job and serious about staying in your field, both of which will show your employer that you are a good employee, worth investing in.

Also, try to get as much professional development as possible. Some employers will offer this as a form of job incentive or will ask you to take a certain number of classes per year. If this is not possible, try to learn as much as you can from senior or more skilled employees. You can do this informally through making friendships, or in a more formal way by asking someone you respect to mentor you.

As you show that you are continually growing your knowledge and skills, this will enable you to qualify for a promotion when it comes available.

Get Recommendations

Getting recommendations from coworkers and supervisors can be very helpful in advancing your career as well, whether you are planning to stay at your current employer or go to a new one. In the past, we would ask for letters of recommendation only when leaving a job.

These days, it is easy to get recommendations through LinkedIn. If you are not familiar with LinkedIn, I recommend you look. It is a professional networking website that is like FaceBook. You can put your resume on the site, connect with coworkers, supervisors, and people with similar professional interests.

When you start a new job, it is a good idea to friend some of your coworkers on LinkedIn. Then, when you have worked on a big project with someone, you can ask them if they are willing to trade recommendations. This is a great way to have some references on your page, so that when you are applying for a promotion or a new job, they will already be there. Also, being proactive and updating your page regularly can help to alleviate some of the stress of needing to ask for recommendations when you do need to look for a job, since they will already be there.

It is a great idea to look for your college professors or classmates on LinkedIn and ask them for recommendations as well. This shows that you have taken your education seriously and done well in classes. Keeping in touch with people on a professional basis can help you to advance your career in the future, because networking is a great way to get new job opportunities. Someone may remember working with you in the past, and then think of you when a new position comes available at their job.

Get a new certification

Another way to increase your income, either at your current job or by applying for a new job, is to get an additional certification. Depending on your field, you may want to take an Associates, Bachelors, Master's degree, or a certificate program. This will typically allow you to make more money since it shows that you have a higher degree of skill or knowledge in your field.

If you are looking to get into a different field, going back to school may be a good way to get started with that as well. The more education you can get, the better. Education can open doors in many ways, by showing you are willing to be a lifelong learner and develop new skills. It also shows that you are dedicated and proactive in your career, which is always a positive thing.

Get a side hustle

If you need more money right away, and can't wait to get a promotion, raise, or new certification then a side hustle might be the right way for you to go. It can also be helpful because most of the time you get to choose your own hours.

Depending on your skillset, there are many different apps and websites that allow you to pick up extra work for cash on your own schedule.

One of the most popular side jobs these days is delivering food. There are many different services that deliver food from restaurants or grocery stores to people's homes. You will just need to have a vehicle, and some extra time to be able to do this. Some examples of apps that you can sign up for to deliver food are Door Dash, Uber Eats, Insta Cart, and Grub Hub.

If you like to drive, you can also do ride sharing. This is where you basically offer your car as a taxi service. Your app will tell you that someone needs to be picked up, what time, and where they are going. This is popular if you live near a downtown area and people want to go out to bars and clubs, or if you live near an airport and people are leaving to travel. You will just need to make sure that you have a driver's license and that you keep your car clean. Some popular apps for this are Uber and Lyft. When you sign up they will just ask you some questions about your vehicle, and have you submit a copy of your driver's license.

There are other apps and websites where you can do freelance work, depending on your skills and occupation. You can do writing, editing, IT work, legal work, move furniture, and many more. You can sometimes find these opportunities on typical job sites under "part time" or you can use sites that are specific to freelancing.

According to The Balance Careers, the best websites to find freelance in 2021 are:

- **Best Overall:** Upwork
- **Best for Graphic Design:** 99designs
- **Best for IT:** FlexJobs
- **Best for Writers:** Freelance Writing Gigs
- **Best for Low Fees:** Craigslist
- **Best for Beginners:** Fiverr

These websites all function slightly differently. Some will allow you to post your resume, and then jobs will contact you. Others have employers post ad's to which you will respond. Whichever you choose, it will allow you to make extra money on your own schedule.

If you are crafty, you can also sell products that you have handmade on Etsy. This allows you to sell things you have already made, or to take custom orders. This is a great way to make money by doing something that you already enjoy.

Conclusion.

This chapter has covered the basics of personal finance, which should get you well on your way to getting your finances under control. Once you have used all of these tips to get your bills paid up to date and have started a savings plan, and made a career plan, you can feel much less stressed out about money.

For specific financial advice it may help to talk to your bank or a financial planner!

Create a Schedule and Routine.

The next aspect of improving your mental health is creating a schedule and routine for yourself and your family. Uncertainty contributes to a large amount of our life stress. So, when we can create a predictable day, it helps to alleviate a large amount of stress by planning ahead of time. In addition, when kids know what to expect throughout the day, it helps them feel secure, and more likely to do what they know will come next (hopefully with less arguing!).

Schedule planning

As busy moms, having a schedule can help us manage our time better and get more done during the day. Organizing life with kids can feel like a daunting task, but if you create a predictable schedule, it really helps the whole family.

We all know how messy it can be to juggle kids' activities, appointments, work, and a seemingly endless To Do list. Being able to prioritize tasks effectively instead of wasting time staring at a mountain of things that needs to be done can help us get started more quickly, without being demoralized by the sheer number of things that need to be done in the day.

Here are some tips that have worked out well for our family. In a house with two working parents, a toddler, and teens, there is always a ton going on in our lives.

Sharing a Calendar.

One of the things that has helped our family to organize our time better is by using a shared calendar. There are a lot of ways you can do this now, from having a paper calendar in an easy to see place, to using technology to assist in scheduling.

What has worked well for us, is to share our Outlook calendars. We sync all our calendars, and upload to our Smart Refrigerator, so the calendar is easily visible. It also sends text reminders of important events and tracks my daughter's work schedule.

Typically, Outlook is what I use for work already, so I have all my meetings and tasks calendared. If you use Apple or Google, you can sync calendars with those as well.

Before we started sharing a calendar, I was forever texting my teen daughter to find out what time she got off work, or when she would be back from her dad's house, so that we could plan dinners for the week.

Sometimes things would slip through the cracks, like remembering to schedule a dentist appointment, the school play, or a friend's birthday party.

Personal Schedule.

For my personal calendar, I block out all my meetings and appointments in Outlook. I also set aside time in my calendar for tasks that I need to accomplish. I can set reminders for due dates for my work tasks, when reports need to be submitted, and use a task list feature. Outlook is great because it has a web app, and you can sync multiple email accounts to view in one place.

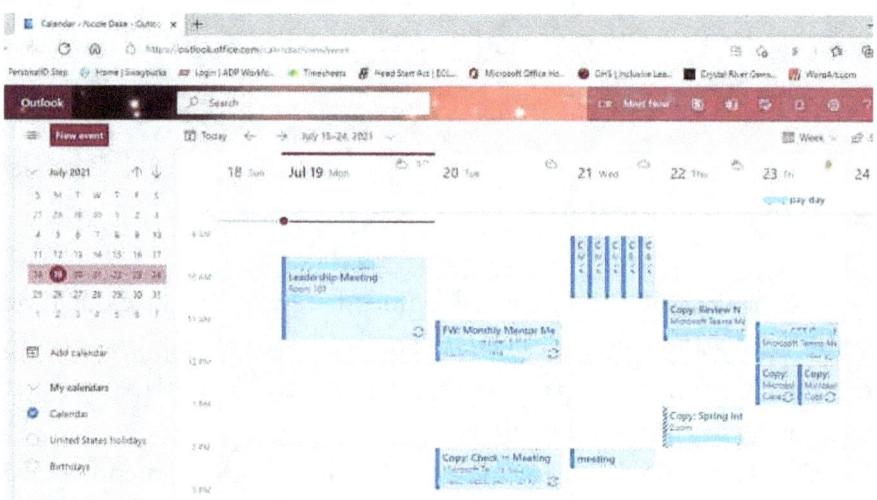

If you are a Gmail or Apple user, there is similar functionality for those as well, as long as everyone is using the same app. Both Outlook mail and Google mail are free as well, so that makes them both budget friendly options. You may want to check what each of your family members is already using, to streamline the process.

Additional To-Do list items, such as my blog post topics, I write in a planner. This can also be helpful for writing down reminders of the big chores that need to be done around the house, like winterizing, changing air filters, or remembering to blow out the sprinklers. I keep a planner book on my desk for work items, and we have a note pad on the refrigerator for the grocery list and shared reminders.

Daily Routine.

With kids especially, having a predictable routine helps to ease their transitions between activities, and reduces melt downs when it is time to stop a fun activity and get other things done. For kids, having a routine can reduce anxiety and help them to feel safe and secure.

Morning Routine

The way our morning goes can determine a lot about the rest of our day. If you wake up late and struggle to get the kids out the door, there is a pretty good chance that you are going to spend the rest of the day feeling stressed.

When we wake up, our bodies already are producing extra Cortisol (the stress hormone) because it helps kick our bodies into gear. Adding extra stress to our morning is never a good thing. Taking time to ease into the day and do things to make yourself in a good mood is crucial.

A good morning routine is important both for us as moms, and for our kids too!

Wake Up Earlier

I'm not a morning person, so this is a habit I have had to learn in my 30's. I used to sleep in until the last possible moment, then roll out of bed and get out the door in about 30 minutes. Not anymore.

The main reason that I started getting up earlier is so that I can have time to get organized and have time for my mental and physical wellness first thing. I like having more time to get ready in the morning so that I don't have to feel like I am in a hurry. Taking time to slow down really sets a more positive tone for my day instead of trying to race against the clock.

These days, since I work from home, I get up at 6am to start work at 8am. When I had to commute, I had to get up earlier.

By alleviating the need to be in a hurry, we can get our minds and bodies set for a productive and pleasant day. Setting yourself up for success helps me to relax and be less stressed throughout the day, instead of feeling like I am constantly running late and playing catch-up.

As I get older, having my day get off to a good start has become more important than that extra hour of sleep. I am more constructive and have a better overview of my day, less stress as I arrange to-do items that I might have forgotten otherwise. Or simply the worry if there was something I hadn't remembered.

Take Time for Yourself

I start the morning with half an hour of yoga, followed by coffee and a shower.

As a busy mom, having that quiet time in the morning really helps me to be mentally relaxed, revitalized, and prepared for the start of the day. Yoga has helped me to feel more chill, than my usually anxious self. That calm helps me to do better when I dive into the rest of my day.

There may be other things you want to incorporate here, such as journaling, a gratitude practice, or saying affirmations.

Practicing self-care is important for our mental health and overall well-being, and by putting your self-care routine first thing in the morning, it isn't something that gets overlooked when you are busy later in the day.

As a toddler mom, having a shower alone also feels like a self-indulgent luxury, and lets me have time for my skincare routine without worrying about my daughter slathering expensive face cream all over her body.

My partner has a different morning routine, and while I am doing yoga and journaling, he has time to himself too. He watches the news, checks email, has coffee on the patio, and calls his mom overseas.

The time you take for yourself can look different for everyone, it is just important that you start the day with something that you enjoy without constantly having to rush.

River Eating her fruits for breakfast.

Getting the kids ready.

After I am ready I get my toddler up. I also dedicate an hour in my schedule to getting her ready, even though with my partner and I working together, it doesn't really take that long. Having that hour means she has time to eat seconds on her breakfast, watch cartoons, and go through three different outfits to find the right one.

We let her start the day slowly too. That makes her less stressed and lets her have time to be ready for the day. Giving her that extra time helps her listen better too when it is time to get out the door.

Our toddler used to rush out the door and have breakfast at daycare, but they started to have breakfast earlier, so we let her have breakfast at home now. Usually she has some fruit, and cereal or pancakes. When she eats at home, we know she is eating something healthy. We also don't have to hurry her out the door at a certain time and we can be more flexible with our schedule.

Once she eats breakfast, we get her dressed, and put her hair into a ponytail, so that it isn't getting a mess during the day. We even have time for her to take a bath or shower if she wants one that day.

After she gets ready, her dad takes her to daycare, and I start work.

Slow Down.

It can be hard to focus on the bigger picture sometimes when you have kids, because it seems like there is always something crazy happening. It is important to at least have in the back of your mind what kind of habits you want your kids to develop. Having a peaceful morning helps and that is something I want my kids to internalize.

In this busy world, it seems like we are always rushing around, and that contributes to our stress in a big way. Getting up a little earlier so that we don't have to be in a hurry is something that has made an impact in my life, and I hope it will for you too!

Find What Works.

You can structure your morning routine any way that works for you, and it may take some trial and error to figure out what is the best way to do things. And since kids are unpredictable and ever changing, be prepared to keep tweaking things as you go along.

We were struggling with getting our 4-year-old to get ready in the morning because she refused to get her clothes on, one day, I decided to brush her hair before she got dressed. When I was done, I told her that she needed to put her shirt on before I made her hair in a ponytail. It worked like a charm!

I also decided to move her vitamins to the bedtime routine when she started taking melatonin for her sleep, so that I wasn't having to remember to do it twice a day.

Sometimes, she will tell me that she wants to do yoga with me in the morning, so I get her up an hour earlier with me. It takes away my quiet time but seeing how cute she is doing the poses more than makes up for that. Plus, it is helping her develop a healthy habit that could last a lifetime, and I don't want to take that away.

A daily routine is just as important for us as moms, because when we automate some of the steps we must do in the day, it can reduce stress for us as well, and help us to be more productive.

After I get ready and get my toddler off to daycare, I sit down with my laptop to check my emails and calendar for what meetings I have. After that, I will start on my daily task list.

What Task to Tackle First?

Once you have completed your morning routine, and are ready to start work for the day, you may be asking yourself which task to tackle first. It has been shown in many research studies that it is best to start with the most difficult task on your list first thing in the morning.

"The harder a task is, the more energy and focus we need to complete it. It therefore makes sense to do the hardest and most important tasks early because starting them when you are tired is more difficult and often results in putting them off for another day." (5 Reasons to do that Hard Task Early (innerdrive.co.uk))

Completing your most difficult task first thing in the morning can also help reduce your overall anxiety level, because you aren't dreading all day that you will have to complete that task.

When I was working in an office environment, I would always return my phone messages first thing in the morning. For some reason I irrationally hate returning phone messages, because I don't really know how time consuming it will be, and many times callers didn't leave the reason for their call, which would be highly anxiety producing for me.

There are always things that come up that I like to call "putting out fires" which is basically things that come up as an emergency that must be prioritized before everything else on your list. Because of this, I usually block off the first half of Monday for such unpredictable events.

Conversely, by Friday afternoons, we are usually out of energy to get anything difficult done. I usually use Friday afternoons for tying up loose ends. I organize my calendar and to-do list for the following week and sync up my calendar to the family calendar.

My kids heading to bed.

Evening Routine.

Having an evening routine may be less important than your morning routine since you are less strapped for time. However, I have found that even if you keep some things a bit more flexible, an overall structure does help, especially when it comes to bedtime for little ones.

After work, I go pick my toddler up from daycare. I ask her about her day and listen to the fun stories about what she did on the way home. Then, I let her pick out what she wants to do and spend about an hour doing something fun with her.

Sometimes, we play outside, or make a craft or recipe, other times we relax on the couch and watch cartoons. I make this a time that is about her, without my devices on.

Then, we will make something for dinner, to have ready when her dad and sister get home from work. We try to eat dinner as a family most days, so that we can catch up with each other after a busy day of going in different directions. It helps us to reconnect too, since this is a time we can talk together while relaxing and enjoying a meal.

After dinner, we usually pick out a movie to watch together, and relax and unwind on the couch.

Finally, we start our nighttime routine. For me and my partner, that consists of cleaning the kitchen, putting food away, and making coffee for the next day.

While one of us is cleaning, the other gets our toddler ready for bed. We get her pajamas on, take her vitamins, feed her fish, and give her sister a good night hug.

Then we read a bedtime story snuggled up in bed, and turn in.

What about the weekend?

How should you schedule your weekend? This will probably depend on several factors:

1. Do you work on the weekend?
2. Do your kids participate in sports or weekend extra curriculars?
3. Do you have errands that have to be done on the weekend?

In our house we usually start out Saturday morning with cleaning up around the house so that we have a "clean slate" for the weekend. Then, my partner and I talk through what needs to be done that weekend over some coffee on the patio.

If your kids participate in any kind of team sports, you know that your weekend will probably be structured around their practice and game schedule.

Both of my kids have taken gymnastics and swimming lessons over the years, and as a more seasoned mama, I learned that even though the 8am class makes it seem like you will get more done, it is better to do 10am or later.

There are a couple of reasons for this. First, I like to have my "me time" in the morning. It helps me feel more in control of my day, not like I am rolling out of bed to get the kids ready and shove them out the door.

Second is for the kids themselves. Kids these days are always on the go, so being able to sleep in a little bit on Saturday morning, or watch cartoons in their pajamas, helps them not to feel rushed either. Childhood is supposed to be fun and when we leave room for a little bit of spontaneity, it helps kids to relax too.

If you have errands to run on the weekend that can monopolize a lot of time too. Especially if you have to bring the kids with you, it can be pretty tiring.

We try to usually limit to just a couple of errands each day on the weekend, so that we do still have a little time to relax. Sometimes it is the grocery store, or the hardware store to pick something up for house and yard work. Then, of course, comes the work itself.

These days, I try to have things delivered if possible. I don't really need to look at light bulbs or a bag of dirt to figure out which is the right one. Also, I don't have to drag bored kids through the store. Which greatly reduces my stress level.

Have fun routines too!

Whether it is Friday night drinks with the neighbors around the grill, or Sunday morning brunch, having routines to look forward to helps you get through the week more easily.

I always try to pick one day out of the weekend to take my kids to do something fun for them. Whether it is the park, a museum, the Zoo, or a trampoline park, having a couple hours to do something new can help kids learn about the world and to relax a bit.

You can also try setting aside one weeknight for a game night, movie night, or pizza night. We do take out on Friday nights to get a break from cooking, and let our toddler pick what she wants to have when we pick her up from daycare.

Conversely, try not to be negative about Monday mornings. These are habits that our children carry with them and can create a negative outlook towards work life.

See a therapist.

Another good way to improve your mental health is by seeing a therapist. Therapy today isn't just for mental health disorders, it can be for anyone who needs a compassionate, listening ear. When you see a professional, you can get medication if needed, as well as learning coping strategies for your stressors. It also can help you enjoy your time with your friends or significant other since you don't need to spend the whole time venting your frustrations.

Going to therapy before you have a breakdown is the same type of preventative care that I spoke about previously, in regard to going to your primary care doctor. Taking care of your mental health is just as important as taking care of your physical health, so it is important to see a professional for mental health issues as well.

Benefits of Therapy

There are many mental health benefits of seeing a therapist. According to Healthline,

> *"Talk therapy encourages open and honest dialogue about issues that cause you distress. Through your relationship with your therapist, you'll work to identify and understand how these stressors are impacting your life, plus develop strategies to manage the symptoms.*
>
> *If you're still on the fence about the benefits of talk therapy, consider this: About 75 percent of people who participate in talk therapy experience some benefit, according to the American Psychological Association."*

You can either go to individual therapy, couples therapy, or family therapy. This will depend on what type of stress or issues that you are experiencing. If you are worried about money, your career, or daily overwhelm, individual therapy may be best. However, if you are experiencing relationship problems, it may be useful to go to either family or couple's therapy.

According to Healthline, some of the benefits of therapy also include:

- help improve communication skills
- help you feel empowered
- empower you to develop fresh insights about your life
- learn how to make healthier choices
- develop coping strategies to manage distress

When you talk to a therapist to develop these new skills it can help you look at life differently. Therapists can teach you how to cope with many daily stressors that you experience and give you space to talk through how you will use your coping skills. As you practice using your new coping skills at home and work, you will become less reactive to things that can make you upset, and look at things from someone else's perspective. This can benefit not only you, but everyone that you have relationships with.

Online Therapy

If you don't feel like you have time to go to a therapist's office, you can also do therapy online, either through zoom or some similar app. This allows you to take less time for your appointments, since you are eliminating the travel time or waiting room. You may even be able to take your therapy appointment over lunch at your job.

According to Healthline, some of the best online therapists in 2021 include:

- **Best overall:** Talkspace
- **Largest network of licensed counselors:** BetterHelp
- **Best online therapy for cognitive behavioral therapy (CBT):** Online-Therapy.com
- **Best online therapy for mental and physical health:** Amwell
- **Best for online psychiatry:** MDLive
- **Best online therapy for your budget:** 7 Cups
- **Best online therapy for couples:** ReGain
- **Best online therapy for teens:** Teen Counseling
- **Best online therapy for LGBTQ:** Pride Counseling
- **Best online therapy for single video sessions:** Doctor on Demand

If you try going to a therapist, you may find it to be very helpful, even if you don't have a mental health disorder. Focusing on your mental wellness is important, and therapy can give you tools to do this more easily in your daily life.

Practice Meditation or Mindfulness.

Practicing Meditation or Mindfulness can help your mental health as well. According to Chester County Hospital, mindfulness can Relieve stress, Lower blood pressure, Reduce chronic pain, Treat heart disease, Boost the immune system, Alleviate stomach problems, Improve sleep (which benefits both your mental and physical health), Produce endorphins (chemicals in the brain that act as natural painkillers) and improve your quality of life. See again how physical and mental health intertwine? Improving one improves the other.

Mindfulness

Another way to improve your mental health is by practicing mindfulness. Mindfulness can help to counteract our daily stress by bringing us away from worries about both the past and the future and being fully present in the moment. We never seem to worry about what is happening now, we always worry about some possible outcome in the future, or we ruminate about things that we think we should have done differently in the past.

By being mindful, we come into the present moment, and we separate ourselves from our fears and our worries. I experienced this profoundly when I took a coaching program a few months ago that was based on the principles of mindfulness.

What is Mindfulness? According to Mindful.org, "Mindfulness is the basic human ability to be fully present, aware of where we are and what we're doing, and not overly reactive or overwhelmed by what's going on around us.

While mindfulness is something we all naturally possess, it's more readily available to us when we practice daily.

Whenever you bring awareness to what you're directly experiencing via your senses, or to your state of mind via your thoughts and emotions, you're being mindful. And there's growing research showing that when you train your brain to be mindful, you're remodeling the physical structure of your brain.

The goal of mindfulness is to wake up to the inner workings of our mental, emotional, and physical processes."

Mindful Presence (Beginner's Mind)

Learning to practice mindfulness, with life itself, and with our parenting, can counteract our busy culture of being on the phone all the time.

Basics of mindfulness are outlined in Mindful Adventure, "[there are] seven specific attitudes that form a foundation for mindfulness. They apply directly, moment by moment and day by day, as you cultivate and deepen mindfulness. These attitudes are ***non-judging, patience, beginner's mind, trust, non-striving, acceptance*** and ***letting go.*** The attitudes support each other and are deeply interconnected. Practicing one will lead to the others. Your ability to bring these attitudes forward in your mindfulness practice will have a great deal to do with your long-term success and ability to calm your anxious mind."

Today, I am going to focus on the idea of Beginners Mind, which can also be referred to as being mindfully present. It is being in the moment and paying attention only to what is going on around you, without worrying about the future or the past.

According to Mindful Adventure, "When you begin to observe what is here in the present moment, the thinking mind tends to believe it knows all about what is happening, or it tries to control what is happening by desperately seeking more information. The activity of thinking forms as a kind of filter between you and the direct experience and true richness of life as it unfolds moment by moment. To practice beginner's mind means to open to the experience in each moment as if meeting it for the first time. Imagine the wonder of a child as she encounters something for the first time. The first smell of a flower, the first drop of rain, the first taste of an orange; all are experienced without the intermediate layer of thought or comparison to the past. These moments are experienced just as they are, in the now, directly, as smell or touch or taste, as sound or sight. In truth, each moment *is* unique."

To practice Beginner's Mind, is to see the world as a child sees it. How much better to connect with them when you can look at the world with wonder as they do, instead of thinking in the back of your mind about your to-do list.

Non-Judgement

When we have thoughts in our daily life, we tend to judge them immediately as either good or bad. This has to do with our mind's way of creating categories for things, judgement typically allows us to make decisions more quickly. However, when we make these snap judgements, we are not using all of our analytical brain. We are reacting from our "lizard brain" which creates the fight or flight response.

By judging situations quickly, we often miss out on all the facts about either a person or a situation. When we allow ourselves to suspend judgement, to think more slowly and react more mindfully, it allows us to see different perspectives and make better decisions.

According to Mindful Ambition, "mindfulness means paying attention in a particular way: on purpose, in the present moment, and without judgment."

The last part of that definition, non-judgment, means letting go of the automatic judgments that arise in your mind with every experience you have.

Setting down the judging mind, even for a short while, is a refreshing weight off your shoulders.

In practicing non-judgment, there is no longer anything to be done about the present moment. No grasping for more, no resisting what is there, and no ignoring life's experience.

When you stop trying to react to your experience, you can open up to it completely, resting in mindful presence."

Non-judgement is like a combination of acceptance and wonder, seeing things just as they are and accepting them. When we stop focusing only on the judgements, we allow ourselves the openness to see beyond them. We can widen our focus and see more of what is happening around them. It helps us get out of single-minded tunnel vision.

The first time I experienced this myself was when I started riding the bus to work. When I drove, all I saw was right in front of me. I focused on the road, the traffic, and where I was going. But, when I rode the bus, I could look out the window and see what was on the sides of me. I could look at the scenery that I had gone past 100's of times before, and never noticed. When we are mindful, we allow ourselves to see more of the world, instead of narrow things that conform to our judgements.

Benefits of Mindfulness

There are additional benefits of mindfulness, in addition to reducing your stress level. It can also be a practice that helps you to be more in tune with yourself, and to live your best life.

According to Mindful.org, "Stress reduction is often an effect of mindfulness practice, but the ultimate goal isn't meant to be stress reduction. The goal of mindfulness is to wake up to the inner workings of our mental, emotional, and physical processes.

Mindfulness trains your body to thrive: Athletes around the world use mindfulness to foster peak performance—from university basketball players practicing acceptance of negative thoughts before games, to BMX champions learning to follow their breath, and big-wave surfers transforming their fears. Seattle Seahawks Coach Pete Carroll, assisted by sports psychologist Michael Gervais, talks about coaching the "whole person." As writer Hugh Delahanty illustrates, players learn a blend of mindfulness, which Gervais calls tactical breathing, and cognitive behavioral training to foster what he calls "full presence and conviction in the moment."

Mindfulness boosts creativity: Whether it's writing, drawing, or coloring, they all have accompanying meditative practices. We can also apply mindfulness to the creative process.

Mindfulness strengthens neural connections: By training our brains in mindfulness and related practices, we can build new neural pathways and networks in the brain, boosting concentration, flexibility, and awareness. Well-being is a skill that can be learned."

As I have learned to be more mindful, I have also become happier, less stressed out, and less anxious. I can be in the moment and appreciate the things around me. Being mindful grounds you in where you are and allows you to enjoy life more. You are enjoying life more because you are paying more attention and experiencing life more.

Mindful Parenting.

Being a mindful parent is basically the opposite of being a parent who is distracted or uninvolved. It is using your *mindful presence* to be with your kids and be fully immersed in your experience with them. This allows you to make the time that you spend with them into *quality time*.

When you parent mindfully, it allows your children to feel more connected to you. They feel heard and they feel special. They feel like they are a priority for you because you are willing to put down what you are doing to pay your full attention to them.

According to the Child Mind Institute, the main things that are important for mindful parenting are slowing down and paying attention to your children's needs. This can benefit your children greatly. It also benefits you by creating a calm and less stressed environment in your home.

The Child Mind Institute says that "Your calm response helps kids calm down, too, he notes. "They say, 'Okay, I can trust my parent to be in control, this is a safe environment.' And they feel more secure, and they thrive. So that's another benefit of parents practicing it on their own."

It seems there's no one right way to Parent Mindfully. Happily, there are many right ways. Sometimes the smallest adjustment in a child's schedule can change a whole family's day-to-day life. And sometimes, Dr. Bertin says, "It's as simple as practicing paying full attention to our kids, with openness and compassion, and maybe that's enough at any moment.""

There are huge benefits to our children's health and self-esteem when we parent them with mindful attention. Also, it should not be too hard for us to do. Mindfulness can reduce stress. When we parent mindfully and take ourselves away from screens and immerse ourselves in being with our kids, this allows us to be more playful and have more fun too. Children are happy and creative by nature and taking some of that for ourselves can really help us in addition to them.

Becoming more mindful as parents has many benefits for both us and our children. Mindfulness allows us to focus on the present moment and stop worrying about the past or the future. Being present in the moment allows our kids to feel important and special. It opens the door for them to welcome learning from us.

In addition, we can also learn from our kids through mindfulness. When we are fully immersed in the present moment, we can experience more joy and playfulness, the way that small children already do. Playing with our kids and enjoying the time we spend with them can do so much to enrich our lives through fun.

Conclusion

There are many benefits to mindfulness, when we slow down, stop judging, and take time to appreciate what is around us, we are able to enjoy life more. Mindfulness allows us to separate ourselves from worries about the future, or recriminations about the past. When we can enjoy the present moment, knowing that things are good for that moment, without fears that the good will be lost in the future, we are much more able to live a happy life.

Paying attention to the moment we are in allows ourselves to experience more fully, enjoy more fully, and to life a more enriched life. We notice things we may not have otherwise noticed. We appreciate things we may have previously overlooked. Being present allows us to live life to the fullest.

Meditation

You can also improve your mental health greatly by practicing meditation. Similarly to mindfulness, meditation can help to reduce stress by quieting the mind and helping you to be present in the moment. There are many different forms of meditation and practicing for only a few minutes a day can help to produce these benefits if you are consistent in your practice. According to the Mayo Clinic, "During meditation, you focus your attention and eliminate the stream of jumbled thoughts that may be crowding your mind and causing stress. This process may result in enhanced physical and emotional well-being."

Not only can meditation help to improve your mental health, it can also improve your physical and emotional health. This is another example of the connection between all the aspects of your health.

Some of the mental health benefits of meditation, according to Headspace, are:

- Increased awareness, clarity, compassion
- a sense of calm.
- Reduced anxiety and depression
- Increase in mental resilience

According to the Mayo Clinic, meditation can have the following emotional health benefits:

- Gaining a new perspective on stressful situations
- Building skills to manage your stress
- Increasing self-awareness
- Focusing on the present
- Reducing negative emotions
- Increasing imagination and creativity
- Increasing patience and tolerance

The mind-body connection also makes it possible for meditation to benefit in reducing symptoms of some illnesses. According to the Mayo Clinic, meditation may benefit people with some of the following illnesses:

- Anxiety

- Asthma
- Cancer
- Chronic pain
- Depression
- Heart disease
- High blood pressure
- Irritable bowel syndrome
- Sleep problems
- Tension headaches

All these benefits to your mental, physical and emotional health can make practicing meditation a great way to improve your overall health and happiness.

How to Meditate

Essentially, boiled down to its core, meditation is the simple act of sitting still and breathing. It sounds simple, right?

According to Headspace, "Most meditations begin by sitting in a quiet place, closing the eyes, calming the mind, and focusing on the breath. But there's more to meditating than sitting quietly and breathing. When we meditate, we are essentially cultivating awareness and compassion; we are training the mind to stop being easily distracted and instead be more focused in the present moment. Using the breath as our anchor in the moment, we simply sit and gradually learn to let thoughts and feelings come and go."

Years ago, I studied Buddhist meditation, and in the classes, they told us that the goal isn't to make your thoughts to go away. The goal is to learn to let your thoughts float past, without attaching to them. When you sit in meditation, you focus on your breathing. If you notice that you are thinking, you just label them "thoughts" and go back to focusing on the breath. You don't judge your thoughts as good or bad, and you don't judge yourself for thinking.

Meditation is about learning that you are not your thoughts, you are the watcher of your thoughts. The more you meditate, the easier it will get, and the less you will notice yourself thinking.

Many Styles of Meditation

Although the basics of meditation will be the same no matter what style you choose, there are many different types of meditation. Some are guided meditations, where you will focus on specific imagery. Some meditations you open your eyes, some you close them. But in all meditations, the goal is to focus on your breath, to create space between yourself and your thoughts.

According to Healthline, there are 9 popular styles of meditation:

- mindfulness meditation
- spiritual meditation
- focused meditation
- movement meditation
- mantra meditation
- transcendental meditation
- progressive relaxation
- loving-kindness meditation
- visualization meditation

Each of these types of meditation will have similar benefits to your wellbeing, however a different style may appeal to you based on your personal preferences.

Mindfulness Meditation

According to Healthline, mindfulness meditation is the most popular form of meditation in the western world. It is a traditionally Buddhist practice, based on the principles discussed in the previous chapter. "In mindfulness meditation, you pay attention to your thoughts as they pass through your mind. You don't judge the thoughts or become involved with them. You simply observe and take note of any patterns."

Spiritual Mediation

Spiritual meditation is "similar to prayer in that you reflect on the silence around you and seek a deeper connection with your God or Universe." This can be a popular practice if you are already a religious practitioner, as it will be in tune with your faith.

Focused Meditation

A focused meditation is one that uses either your own senses, or an external object to focus on during the meditation. This can be helpful if you are easily distracted. According to Healthline, "Focused meditation involves concentration using any of the five senses.

For example, you can focus on something internal, like your breath, or you can bring in external influences to help focus your attention.

Try counting mala beads, listening to a gong, or staring at a candle flame."

Movement Meditation

"Although most people think of yoga when they hear movement meditation, this practice may include walking through the woods, gardening, qigong, and other gentle forms of motion." This is a good type of meditation to choose if you prefer being active to sitting still.

Mantra Meditation

This is another form of Buddhist, or Hindu meditation. "This type of meditation uses a repetitive sound to clear the mind. It can be a word, phrase, or sound, such as the popular "Om."

It doesn't matter if your mantra is spoken loudly or quietly. After chanting the mantra for some time, you'll be more alert and in tune with your environment. This allows you to experience deeper levels of awareness."

Transcendental Meditation

Transcendental meditation is similar to mantra meditation. However, "It is more customizable than mantra meditation, using a mantra or series of words that are specific to each practitioner."

Progressive Relaxation

Also called progressive muscle relaxation, "Oftentimes, this form of meditation involves slowly tightening and relaxing one muscle group at a time throughout the body." This allows your body to gradually relax.

Visualization Meditation

"Visualization meditation is a technique focused on enhancing feelings of relaxation, peace, and calmness by visualizing positive scenes or images.

With this practice, it's important to imagine the scene vividly and use all five senses to add as much detail as possible." There are many guided visualization meditations available either as audio books, or on YouTube that you can find for free.

Loving Kindness Meditation

Loving kindness meditation is another type of visualization meditation. "Loving-kindness meditation is used to strengthen feelings of compassion, kindness, and acceptance toward oneself and others.

It typically involves opening the mind to receive love from others and then sending a series of well wishes to loved ones, friends, acquaintances, and all living beings."

Playing music is one of my hobbies.

Pursue Your Hobbies.

Your mental health can also be improved by pursuing your hobbies. When you have a hobby or interest that you are passionate about, it can be therapeutic to spend time doing something that you love. Whether you love baking, chess, crafts, music, games, sports or something else, any of those can help with your personal development and life enjoyment. Also, if you can involve your kids with your hobbies, it can become something special you love to do together.

Hobbies allow you to use your mental energy for something positive that you enjoy, instead of always focusing on your career, money, and to-do list.

According to Head to Health, "Spending time on an activity that you enjoy can improve your mental health and wellbeing. Research shows that people with hobbies are less likely to suffer from stress, low mood, and depression. Activities that get you out and about can make you feel happier and more relaxed. Group activities like team sports can improve your communication skills and relationships with others.

Your interests may be creative, athletic, academic, or something distinctly personal. You may choose a hobby that you can do alone or as part of a group. Whatever your interests are, there is sure to be a hobby out there for you. What matters is that it is something you find meaningful and enjoyable."

If you take time every day or every week to spend on your hobbies, this can make you happier and more relaxed, thereby improving your life.

11

Social Emotional Health

Social Emotional health is the part of your health that is determined by your feelings and relationships. The way you interact with others daily is a big determinant of either your stress level, or your happiness. All of the important relationships with the people in your life can have effects on your social emotional health.

People need other people. We don't live in a vacuum, and we can take on the feelings and emotions of the people around us. When we work to improve ourselves, it can improve our relationships as well. Similarly, when we improve our relationships, we can improve our own happiness with life.

Communication

One of the biggest reasons why things can go badly wrong in any relationship has to do with communication skills. The better we are at communication, the better we are going to be able to navigate all of our relationships. There are many different communication skills, and communications that we can learn about to be able to have more positive relationships.

There are many different guides out there to talk about having positive communications in all of your relationships. Some of the most commonly used communication books to read are Crucial Conversations, and Non-Violent Communication. We all communicate on a daily basis with many people, but we want to make sure that we are communicating in a way that other people will perceive as being positive.

Politeness

One of the key components of communication is politeness. Politeness is important because it shows people that you care about them. Being polite is following social niceties, like saying please and thank you. It can also be communicated in non-verbal ways, like giving up a seat on the bus for someone who appears elderly or handicapped.

Being polite is important because it shows that we are following social contracts, and willing to treat others with courtesy and respect in most life situations. According to LinkedIn Pulse, "Politeness reduces stress in oneself and others. By learning that one can talk to you with respect, you'll be ready to get out of your shell and be willing to mingle with others freely. With free mingling, people can always share their stressful conditions and situations. Politeness will improve productive of a person both at a personal and organizational level as they will feel as valued people. The polite words in an office may seem unnecessary, but they boost the morale and performance of employers and fellow employees."

When we are children, we learn to be polite to others and to use manners. However, with the increasing use of technology, people are interacting face-to-face less and less. This means, we practice manners and politeness less. We sit on our phones when we are waiting in line, instead of talking to someone else. Since we aren't using our manners in social situations as much, that means we need to make a conscious effort to be polite to others when we do interact.

There may also be cultural or generational gaps in manners or politeness. It is especially important to older generations to use manners and politeness, and to act in a more formal way. That is an important way of showing care and respect to others, to be aware of these differences, and when you are unsure to default to a more formal way of speaking.

Listening

Listening is another one of the key communication skills. I will always remember in the movie Fight Club a scene when the two main characters are discussing the way that other people listen to them. It is stated that sometimes, people aren't really listening, they are just waiting for their turn to speak. A lot of our communication with people tends to work this way, and that means many times we are not really open to hearing what other people are saying, we are just waiting to tell them our own viewpoint.

Improving our listening skills can go a long way toward understanding other people's perspectives. When we understand, we have more opportunity for caring and compassion, because we are truly being open to another person.

Another important thing to keep in mind is that if you want to really listen to someone, it can help to be mindfully present with them. We have discussed Mindful Presence in an earlier chapter, and in this case, it can also mean putting away all distractions when you talk to someone. Turn off the TV, put down your phone, and look at them directly. This shows that you value someone because you are willing to give them your full attention.

There are two main types of listening skills that are popular today and can help us to improve our listening to others: Active Listening, and Transformational Listening.

Active Listening

Active listening is a way of showing that you are attentively listening to, and engaging with, the person that you are speaking with. This is especially popular in business communication settings, but it can apply to any conversation that you have with someone.

According to Very Well Mind, "Active listening refers to a pattern of listening that keeps you engaged with your conversation partner in a positive way. It is the process of listening attentively while someone else speaks, paraphrasing and reflecting back what is said, and withholding judgment and advice."

Very Well Mind goes on to say,

> *"Active listening involves more than just hearing someone speak. When you practice active listening, you are fully concentrating on what is being said. You listen with all of your senses and give your full attention to the person speaking.*
>
> *Below are some features of active listening:[1]*

- *Neutral and nonjudgmental*
- *Patient (periods of silence are not "filled")*
- *Verbal and nonverbal feedback to show signs of listening (e.g., smiling, eye contact, leaning in, mirroring)*
- *Asking questions*
- *Reflecting back what is said*
- *Asking for clarification*
- *Summarizing*

> *In this way, active listening is the opposite of passive hearing."*

Being active instead of passive is very important because it allows the speaker to feel valued, and to know that you are really listening, instead of just waiting for your turn to speak. When we are actively listening, it also can create a sense of trust so that the speaker will be more willing to open up and share what is really on their mind and in their heart.

Showing that you really care for someone, and their opinions through active listening creates space for a real dialogue to occur, instead of just people talking at each other or over each other. When this happens, there is a more honest sharing of ideas and feelings, because people feel safe in the conversation, and they are bound to be less reactive or defensive. This allows for better collaboration or compromise. It also will allow difficult conversations to flow more smoothly.

Transformational Listening

Another type of listening that allows the speaker to feel valued in a conversation is called Transformational Listening. This type of listening is different than Active Listening, in that you don't ask questions while someone is talking, you use more nonverbal cues to let them know that you are engaged and present.

According to Dr. Robin Johnson,

> "Transformational Listening demonstrates respect behaviorally, helps you collaborate, builds trust, balances extraversion-introversion and direct-indirect communication styles, and is one of the most powerful competencies in the multicultural leader's toolkit.
>
> It is different from active listening since the listener refrains from asking questions or talking while listening to others. The intent of the listener is to connect, demonstrate respect, and learn from the other while the listener provides the speaker(s) with their undivided caring attention. It is one way of listening that can be used in addition to (or instead of) active listening."

Transformational listening focuses on listening with an open heart, and not forming an opinion until the speaker has finished speaking. You will give them your full attention and mirror their affect so that they will know that you are engaged. Then, when the first person has finished speaking, you can ask them a question or state your opinion. It focuses on taking turns and giving everyone space to speak. This practice can show respect and care in a one-on-one situation, and inclusiveness in a group setting.

Over the summer I took a class that focused heavily on Transformational Listening, and since then I have been using these principles into practice. In my experience, it has been very similar to the practice of mindful presence, which we discussed earlier. When we practice transformational listening, we listen without judging. We simply listen to the speaker in an open way. We wait for them to finish before we begin to say something ourselves.

By listening fully and attentively this way, I have found that I have better conversations with my children and my partner. It can help people not to talk over each other, because each person has space to communicate their points. Listening can help to improve all aspects of our relationships, not just our conversations themselves, because truly being listened to is so rare and therefore valuable. Listening to someone can help them to know that you value them, and that you consider the relationship to be important.

Fundamental Attribution Error

Another method for improving our communication is to become aware of the Fundamental Attribution Error. The fundamental attribution error is a psychological term that refers to always seeking a negative bias in your thinking. It means, when someone does something that upsets you, then you will automatically think that they did it purposely to hurt you, without giving them the benefit of the doubt.

An example of this I used with my daughter is when someone cuts you off in traffic, to automatically assume that they are a bad person and don't care about your feelings. I let her know there are plenty of other reasons this could happen. They could be distracted, in a hurry, or a new driver. It is possible that someone had an emergency and is rushing home to deal with it, so they are driving in a more aggressive manner than usual.

According to the Harvard Business School Online,

> *"The fundamental attribution error refers to an individual's tendency to attribute another's actions to their character or personality, while attributing their behavior to external situational factors outside of their control. In other words, you tend to cut yourself a break while holding others 100 percent accountable for their actions.*
>
> *For instance, if you've ever chastised a "lazy employee" for being late to a meeting and then proceeded to make an excuse for being late yourself that same day, you've made the fundamental attribution error.*
>
> *The fundamental attribution error exists because of how people perceive the world. While you have at least some idea of your character, motivations, and situational factors that affect your day-to-day, you rarely know everything that's going on with someone else. Similar to confirmation and overconfidence biases, its impact on business and life can be reduced by taking several measures."*

By being aware of the fundamental attribution error, we can be more compassionate with others, and ask about their motives behind their actions, instead of making assumptions. Often our assumptions are wrong, and people seldom do things for the nefarious reasons that we imagine. By taking ourselves out of the imaginary story and asking people for their perspective or the truth of the situation, we will have better relationships with others. When people feel *seen* and *heard*, they are less likely to be defensive, and there is an opportunity for understanding and improved relationships.

When we look for the real story behind someone's actions instead of jumping to assumptions based on the fundamental attribution error, it allows us to see and understand people more fully. Knowing a true reason why something happened can help us to avoid anger, resentment, irritation and making snap judgements of other people.

Crucial Conversations

Some conversations are more difficult, and more important than others. This type of conversation can be referred to as a Crucial Conversation because there is something riding on the outcome. For example, if a couple is talking about divorce or reconciliation, this would be a crucial conversation.

There is a book with this same title that explains skills that can be used to navigate crucial conversations. According to the book's description,

"Crucial Conversations gives you the tools you need to step up to life's most difficult and important conversations, say what's on your mind, and achieve the positive resolutions you want. You'll learn how to:

- *Prepare for high-impact situations with a six-minute mastery technique*
- *Make it safe to talk about almost anything*
- *Be persuasive, not abrasive*
- *Keep listening when others blow up or clam up*
- *Turn crucial conversations into the action and results you want*

Whether they take place at work or at home, with your neighbors or your spouse, crucial conversations can have a profound impact on your career, your happiness, and your future. With the skills you learn in this book, you'll never have to worry about the outcome of a crucial conversation again."

Crucial conversations are conversations where there may be a high level of conflict, an important decision to be made, or both. Learning to manage difficult conversations can help us to better navigate our relationships and show people that we care even in the midst of difficult times.

Non-Violent Communication

Another important way to improve your communication is by using a technique known as Non-Violent Communication. Words can be considered violent when they are used in a hurtful manner, such as insulting people, talking down to them, using racial slurs, and things of this nature. Similarly, communication can be NON violent when people are kind, ask questions to the other's intent, and use compassion and feelings based statements.

According to the book description,

"Nonviolent Communication, this renowned peacemaker presents his complete system for speaking our deepest truths, addressing our unrecognized needs and emotions, and honoring those same concerns in others. With this adaptation of the best-selling book of the same title, Marshall Rosenberg teaches in his own words how to:

- *Identify the four steps of the Nonviolent Communication process*
- *Employ the four-step Nonviolent Communication process in every dialogue you engage in*
- *Utilize empathy to safely confront anger, fear, and other powerful emotions*
- *Discover how to overcome the blocks to compassion and open to our natural desire to enrich the lives of those around us*

- *Observations, feelings, needs, and requests--how to apply the four-step process of Nonviolent Communication to every dialogue we engage in*
- *Overcoming the blocks to compassion--and opening to our natural desire to enrich the lives of those around us*
- *How to use empathy to safely confront anger, fear, and other powerful emotions."*

Non-Violent Communication provides us with an opportunity to be able to show a calm state, understand other's emotions, and avoid placing blame. When we talk using our own feelings and experiences as a background for what we are asking someone, it shows others that we are willing to be open, honest, and non-judgmental with other people. This allows them to respond in a similar way without allowing their feelings to cloud their judgement and get defensive.

Learning to say no and set boundaries.

Setting Boundaries

In addition to improving our communication skills, setting boundaries is a skill that can be useful in all our relationships in life.

Boundaries are areas of your life where you set a standard regarding how you want to be treated by other people. According to Psych Central,

> *"Personal boundaries are simply the lines we draw for ourselves in terms of our level of comfort around others.*
>
> *These boundaries may have to do with:*

- *physical contact (not feeling comfortable hugging a person you've just met)*
- *verbal interactions (not wanting a friend or family member to speak down to you)*
- *our own personal space (choosing to not have others in your home when you aren't there)*

> *These boundaries typically fall into a few specific categories:*

- *emotional (protecting our own emotional well-being)*
- *physical (protecting our physical space)*
- *sexual (protecting our needs and safety sexually)*
- *workplace (protecting our ability to do our work without interference or drama)*
- *material (protecting our personal belongings)*
- *time (protecting the use, and misuse, of our time)*

> *Boundaries can also exist in a variety of situations, including:*

- *at work*
- *at home*

- *when visiting family*
- *when out with friends*

> *Really, any time you are talking about engaging with others, you've likely got personal boundaries that surround that situation."*

Since everyone has different personal boundaries, someone may not know that they have crossed your boundary. When this happens, you have a choice whether you will speak up or not. You can simply allow someone to violate your boundary to keep the peace and tell yourself that it's not that important. Or you can speak up for yourself and tell the other person that they have made you uncomfortable.

Whichever way you decide to go, it can be a stressful situation. Having a boundary crossed can be very upsetting, since someone has treated you in a way that you believe to be hurtful. However, we can also be afraid to speak up for ourselves too, and it can be very stressful to speak up for yourself. This can be especially true if you have been brought up to believe that group peace is more important than your own rights.

According to Healthline,

> *"Boundaries protect relationships from becoming unsafe. In that way, they actually bring us closer together than farther apart, and are therefore necessary in any relationship," says Melissa Coats, a licensed professional counselor.*
>
> *Having boundaries allows you to make yourself a priority, whether that's in self-care, career aspirations, or within relationships."*

Every time you enforce a boundary with someone, it will get easier. It is a sign that you value yourself enough to tell someone "no" and put your needs first. Often, if a person has violated a boundary by accident, they will simply apologize and then act differently in the future. That is typically the way that boundaries are treated in respectful relationships.

Most people want others to be comfortable and will do what they can to make that happen.

It is only if the same person starts to continuously violate the same boundary that you may begin to have a bigger problem. For example, I once told my mom that I was trying to set a boundary with someone and she told me, "You don't deserve to have boundaries."

Most people won't tell you in such straightforward language as that, but their actions in continuously violating your boundaries tells you the same thing. They don't think that you deserve to have boundaries. That means, for whatever reason, someone is consistently treating you with disrespect. If this happens, you can tell them "no" more firmly again, or you may need to have one of the Crucial Conversations we talked about earlier to determine why they feel that they can treat you with continued disrespect.

Relationships impact your health and happiness

Just as in the first chapter I noted that Relationships can be one of our main causes of life stress, they can also be one of the main causes for happiness.

According to Psychology Today, "Satisfying relationships not only make us happy, they also influence our long-term health as much as getting enough sleep, eating healthy, and not smoking. Many research studies have shown that satisfying relationships are associated with better health, greater happiness, and even longer life."

Psychology Today goes on to say that, "How does social support impact our health? It seems there are biological, behavioral, and emotional pathways. Partners and friends or family can encourage us by listening, showing that they care, helping our self-esteem, motivating us to be healthy or distracting us from our stressors. On the other hand, criticism and ongoing unresolved conflict can make us feel more stressed and take energy away from managing our problems."

In the following sections I will address many of the relationships that impact our lives daily, and how we can use our communication skills to improve our relationships, and therefore our happiness.

According to one study cited in Psychology Today, "Vaillant found that the ability to be intimate with another person was one of the strongest predictors of health and happiness. Intimacy phobic and commitment phobic individuals were among the most unhappy and discontented individuals. But luckily these attachment patterns are changeable, and many study participants were able to change these patterns at some point in their lifetime....It was also found that romantic love wasn't the only predictor of happiness. Other prognosticators included having close relationships with children, parents, siblings, friends and colleagues. So, romantic love is not the only route to happiness. Friendship love, companionate love, parental love and attachment love can get you there as well."

All of the relationships in our lives have the ability to greatly enrich our lives. When we have people in our lives that we love and care about, and that love and care about us in return, it can make us much happier and healthier as well.

Relationship with your Partner.

Our partnered love relationships are often a focal point of our lives. When we get into a long-term relationship, it can give us a sense of safety and security, knowing that we don't face the world alone. However, this also means that when we feel our primary relationship is threatened, we can respond with strong feelings, because we feel our basic safety and security has been disrupted.

This means, our relationship with our partners can be one of our biggest sources of safety, happiness, and love, or if the relationship is suffering, it can be our biggest source of distress. For this reason, it is very important to make time for your partner, to show them love and care, so that we can have a happy life together, instead of being at odds. The best way to keep our relationship strong is through open communication, as discussed in the previous chapter.

Gary and I at the race track

Dating Relationships

Casual dating relationships can be fun and exciting, and a source of happiness in our lives. However, when we don't feel like our dating expectations or needs are being met, dating can be a cause of stress as well. We all want to be loved and valued, and dating can be a way to fill that need.

When we first start dating, it can be stressful getting to know a new person and deciding if the relationship may be a good fit for our future. As we start dating, we may have different types of relationships that we are looking for. Some people date casually so that they can find a source of light-hearted fun and exploration. They want someone to attend social events with and enjoy meeting new people and going to new places. This type of relationship can be a great source of companionship and fun, without expectations about the future.

Other times, people date so that they can find a potential partner for a long-term relationship. This type of relationship can be seen as more serious, although it can also be a lot of fun. When we date looking for a serious relationship, it is like auditioning someone for a role in a play. Someone dating looking for a long-term relationship will often seek someone with not only similar interests to pursue in the short-term, but also who has similar goals and values. Sharing similar ideas about marriage, children, work, and other important values is what someone is looking for in this type of dating.

The biggest cause of distress in dating relationships can come when two people fall in love but have a different idea of what they want from the relationship. This means, one partner is looking to just casually date and have fun, and the other is looking for a more long-term commitment. A mismatch in desires and expectations can often lead to a breakup because two people are not compatible. Often a breakup, or events leading up to a breakup, can be very stressful and impact our functioning in other areas of our lives.

Another reason that couples may break up is when they find that they have different values and goals. Again, they have discovered that they are just not compatible. This may happen if a couple argues about money, religion, politics, marriage, children or other values and future goals. One person may be a night owl, and the other loves the mornings. One may eat healthy, and the other loves fast food. One may be very religious, and the other is an atheist. One may want children and the other does not. All of these issues can be worked through if the couple wants to commit, but often some of the differences feel like too much, and they will break up because of these differences.

Even though casual dating may be stressful at times, many people find dating and relationships to be one of the main sources of enjoyment in life. Also, not all relationships are doomed to fail in the ways that I have mentioned above, and not all break ups end in tears. Sometimes past partners can make great friends. Other times, a couple will decide that their dating relationship is successful and decide to make a long term commitment.

Transition from casual to long-term relationship

During the transition from a casual to a long-term relationship, it is a good time for a couple to discuss their values and life goals, and expectations of their partners. That way, they can be clear if their ideology and what they want out of life is compatible. It is important to know if your partner is truly compatible before making a long-term commitment.

When you fall in love, the saying that "love is blind" can be very apt. At the beginning of a new relationship, we are still in the honeymoon phase, and we don't always notice the day to day things that are going to be important later in a relationship. This can be especially true before a couple moves in together. They have only seen the best of the other person, and not their worst habits that may have a major impact later on in the relationship.

Prior to getting married, many couples will also go into pre-marriage counseling so that they can have a therapist that is able to help with asking these types of difficult questions.

According to The Knot, "Premarital counseling oftentimes will help couples snuff out potential areas of growth in their relationship, as well as where they most need to align and communicate. Most of the time, it's conducted by a licensed therapist (an LMFT), or a religious leader like a pastor in a church. Some pastors and churches will require premarital counseling in order for a wedding ceremony to be conducted. However, premarital counseling is a platform for couples to have open and honest conversations prior to marriage about real life topics with the help of mediation."

Some of the possible topics that can be discussed during this type of counseling, according to The Knot, may include:

- Communication
- Finances
- Beliefs
- Values
- Roles
- Responsibilities
- Sex and Intimacy
- Family relationships
- Possible children
- Decision-making processes
- Conflicts and results
- Hobbies and leisure time

Talking through these issues, as well as any others that the couple finds to be important, prior to getting married will help the couple to be sure about their decision to marry. This will allow them to find out more about their partner's beliefs, values, and way of life prior to making a lifetime commitment.

Long-Term Relationships

Long term relationships are one of the foundations of our social structure. For hundreds of years, a family has socially been based on marriage and children. Having a long-term partner can be a source of happiness, safety, and security.

As I said in the previous section, many people in the western world date with the intention of finding a marriage partner. After the dating stage, people will often get engaged, married, or move in together. When you live with someone day in and day out, you can share a deep relationship.

Often, people will see finding a life partner as one of their major goals. People want to fall in love, get married, and sometimes have a family. This is seen as socially acceptable to do in many parts of society. People want to get married and have a stable relationship as the basis for a happy life.

According to the APA, "It's not marriage that makes you happy, it's happy marriage that makes you happy, Gilbert said. Married people are happier than unmarried ones, perhaps because the single best predictor of human happiness is the quality of social relationships."

Having a long-term partner can increase your life satisfaction if you have a good relationship. A good partnership is like a team, where you always have someone in your corner to help you and cheer you on with your achievements

A healthy relationship can be a cause of deep life satisfaction for many years. Having a partner who loves, accepts, and appreciates you can give you an overall sense of safety and happiness. This will allow you to have more resilience against difficult situations as well. Working together against a difficult situation can make it feel easier and more manageable.

So, what makes a marriage a good one? According to Health Prep, "Many abilities can help a marriage succeed, however, the best ability is availability. When you make time for each other, the relationship will naturally get stronger." By spending more time together, you can strengthen your marriage. When you make yourself available to your partner, you are showing that you value them, and that they are a priority to you. Giving your valuable time to your partner can help to make your relationship stronger and happier.

Partners with relationships that work can communicate with each other effectively throughout their day and come to a deep level of understanding and commitment. According to Health Prep, "Open, honest, and healthy communication is to marriage what water is to a garden. When the communication stops or becomes toxic, the marriage will wither away. Communication is easier when we are discussing something positive but strive to be honest and have open communication even during difficult times. Whether you just got a great job offer or are dealing with a financial setback, open communication will make the expectations of each spouse clear and will also help to accept when things fall short of those expectations. And remember, how we say something is just as important as what we say. Try to keep your words kind and constructive."

Using the communication and listening skills from the previous chapter can really help your relationship to flourish. Honesty creates trust, which in turn allows you to continuously be more open in your communication with your partner.

Shared values and goals, making time for self-care, and communicating your expectations about intimacy can also benefit your relationship. All of these are among the items that you may have discussed in pre marriage counseling, but it is good to keep an open dialogue about anything that is important to your relationship, including the relationship itself. A feeling of teamwork and cooperation can help to keep your marriage happy as well.

My partner will say to me, "are we an effective team?" and it is very reassuring to me. We are solutions-oriented people, and when a problem comes up, it is us working as a team against the problem, instead of blaming each other for the problem and fighting about it. Working together is very important to make a relationship last.

That is not to say there won't be any conflict. Every relationship is bound to have conflict and disagreements, it is how you handle them that is important. When you show love and compassion even during a disagreement, that is important to showing that you care more about your relationship than your viewpoint about a specific issue. This is an instance where communication is key. It is important to practice non-violent communication and crucial conversation principles, so that even in a disagreement you can still know that you are a team.

When we listen attentively and with an open heart, even during a disagreement, then we show that we care about the other person. Showing that attention and willingness to listen to another's perspective allows the relationship to deepen once the argument has been resolved by both people. Sometimes this can take the form of a compromise, or a collaboration to find a solution to a problem. It is important that when you resolve a disagreement that you will find a solution that is acceptable to both of you.

Some arguments are difficult and might not be resolved right away. In that case, it is alright to set the issue aside, think it through individually, and talk about it again later, once you have calmed down. This space to think, can sometimes allow one or both partners to come up with a solution that wasn't obvious in the heat of the moment. That is why it is important not to always let your feelings of the moment cloud your judgement. You can talk about your feelings openly and honestly, but without blaming the other person.

Blame and judgement are two of the surest ways to make an argument last a long time and end on a bad note.

However, when you have relationship drama, or are constantly arguing with your partner, it can lead to a good deal of unhappiness instead.

Something that many young lovers don't realize is that besides being in a love relationship, a marriage is also like a business deal. Most couples will live together, intermingle their finances, and perhaps have children, pets or own a house together. This means, since so much of their lives are intertwined, it is important to have shared values, as well as a shared goal for the future. When people live together and realize that their goals and values no longer align, this can often lead to a painful divorce.

When a couple divorces, it isn't a simple emotional break up like with casual dating. During a divorce, people are in a great deal of emotional pain, but there are many practical issues that are needed to be dealt with as well. Finances and property need to be divided, and the former couple will need to decide where children and pets will live. Trying to separate an intermingled life is very difficult, time consuming, and emotionally fraught.

During a divorce, someone's overall life satisfaction plummets, and it can be a huge cause of stress and sadness, sometimes for years.

Since divorce can have such a negative impact on all areas of your life, it is important to make sure that you are really on the same page with your partner prior to committing to a marriage. It is much easier to "survive" a breakup when you are in the casual dating stage, vs. once you have been married for some time. That is why it is so important to have the difficult conversations up front, so that you will be able to realize if you are not long-term compatible as a couple.

My friend Kelly and I

Relationships with Friends.

Our friendships can contribute greatly to our social-emotional health and happiness as well. Making time in our busy schedules for our friends is important. They say it takes a village to raise a child, and your friends are your village. Friendships can help you have fun and relax, as well as enjoying conversation and hobbies together. Maintaining friendships after motherhood can help you feel like you are retaining an important piece of yourself that may sometimes easily get lost.

Friendships can enrich our lives in many ways, and even when you are in a committed relationship and have children, it is still important to have friends. Firstly, it allows you to have another person to talk with besides your partner, and that way you are not placing all of your social needs onto them and becoming a burden. When you only talk to your partner, it can make your world very small.

When we have friends, it allows us to learn about new and different perspectives, gives us new ideas, and helps us to explore the wider world. There are many different ways to meet new friends, from places we like to go and common interests, or by proximity and being at a similar place in life. For example, if we are always at the gym, we can make friends at the gym.

If you are wanting to seek out new friendships, you can meet them online through social media if you look for local meetup groups. Some groups will be interest-based, such as a church or a hobby. Sometimes, you will be able to meet other moms, or other people with similar jobs. Whatever way you decide to network, it is always good meeting new people, and learning about what others have to offer.

Friends can provide us with fun and companionship, they can help us learn new things, and they can help us in a time of need. It can be good to meet your neighbors, at different places like the dog park, bars, health clubs, or other community centers. It is great to have friends that live nearby that you can spend time with on a regular basis. You can also meet friends through your kids' activities, and socialize with other families that way.

Work or School Relationships.

Relationships at work and school can allow us to express ourselves differently than in a personal space. They allow us to showcase our expertise and use our intellect. When we excel in work or school, it allows us to take a sense of pride and purpose in what we do. Supportive work and school relationships help us aim for high goals, and to form a collaborative work environment. Having positive work and school relationships is also important just because of the sheer amount of time that we spend in both and having friends or co-workers with a shared experience can help us feel supported.

It is especially important to have good work relationships because we spend so much of our time at work. Communication in a professional business manner is very important to ensure that we are creating positive professional relationships. Many of the communication, politeness and listening skills are great to apply at work, so that we can form collaborative working relationships with the people that you see every day.

Relationships with Kids.

Our relationships with our kids are also important to our social-emotional health, as we are to theirs. Improving our relationships with our kids can help to alleviate some of our mom stress, although usually I find that it isn't my kids making me stressed out. Typically, something else stresses us out causing us not to be present with our kids. If we take time to immerse ourselves in a game of hide and seek, playing with bubbles, or building a block tower, that can reduce our stress level too because we are having fun. Fun is a great way to reduce stress.

I know that kids can be very stressful at times too. They have wants, needs, and desires that can be very different from our own. Kids also don't have all the self-monitoring skills that adults have and can become very upset and reactive over things that seem at times very small to us. The red jacket is dirty, or they don't like their dinner. Often, they can have a meltdown over something that we don't think is important at all.

We want our kids to listen, but as discussed in the earlier chapter, we need to be able to listen first, and model good listening skills for them. Everything we want our kids to be able to do, we need to teach them. This includes emotional self-regulation.

When it comes to parenting, our relationship with our children is going to depend a lot on our individual parenting styles. The way we parent, and the way we model our way of living life, is going to make a big difference in our relationships with our children and possibly *their* future relationships as well.

Parenting Styles

Parenting styles can contribute in large part to the way you relate to your child and the quality of the relationships with them as well. Your parenting style refers to the way that you typically interact with your children, how you set rules and follow up on them, how you listen and prioritize your relationship with your child, and many other dynamics that are common to your household.

There are four different parenting styles, all of which have different types of consequences for children as they grow up. It is important to be sure that your parenting style reflects your values and allows you to have the best possible relationship with your child.

The four parenting styles are:

- Authoritarian (or Disciplinarian)
- Permissive (or Indulgent)
- Authoritative
- Neglectful (or Uninvolved)

As you read the following information about each of the parenting styles, you can think about how you raise your children, and about how your parents raised you as well.

Authoritarian Parenting

Many of us will identify this as the style that our own parents had, where they had firm rules that were expected to be obeyed without question.

According to Wellness Mind, "Authoritarian means requiring someone to strictly obey authority without asking too many questions. Do any of these statements match your behavior?

- You believe children should be seen and not heard.
- While setting and implementing the rules, you believe it's "my way or the highway."
- You don't take your child's feelings into consideration.

If any of these statements sound true, you might be an authoritarian parent. In Authoritarian style of parenting, children are expected to follow the strict rules established by the parents."

Authoritarian parenting may make their children feel disempowered later in life, as though what they think or feel is not important, since that is the message that they grew up with.

Permissive Parenting

From first glance, permissive parents might seem like the "fun" parents, because they usually let kids do whatever they want without too much consequence and push back. The main problem with this is that kids gain too much control over their world and can push permissive parents to their whims. This makes children ill prepared to go into the real world, and to be told "no." Typically, children learn to be told no, and understand boundaries early in life.

They learn to understand that actions have consequences. Children of permissive parents don't understand this, and frequently their parents will get them out of any trouble that you get into out in the wider world.

According to Wellness Mind,

> *"Permissive parents set very few boundaries and rules and they are reluctant to enforce rules. These parents are warm and indulgent, but they do not like to say no or disappoint their children. Do any of these statements match your behavior?*

- *You set rules but rarely enforce them.*
- *You don't give out consequences very often.*
- *You think little interference is best for your child.*

> *If those statements sound familiar, you might be a permissive parent. With a permissive parenting style, the parents are lenient. They often only step in when there is a serious issue. Permissive parents believe in the motto "kids will be kids" and are quite forgiving. Permissive parents usually play more of a friend role than a parent role. They often encourage their children to talk with them about their problems and do not put much effort into discouraging bad behavior."*

Later in life, children of permissive parents may struggle with obeying other authority figures and following rules. This is because they haven't had to reliably follow rules in the past, and it can be much more difficult to learn in adulthood.

Authoritative Parenting

After reading the first two parenting styles, authoritative parenting may seem like a middle ground. Parents set rules that they expect children to follow, but they also will explain those rules and prioritize their relationships with their children.

According to Wellness Mind,

"After years of research, child development experts believe that authoritative parenting is the best parenting style among the four styles of parenting. It is a parenting style characterized by high responsiveness and high demands. Authoritative parents are responsive to the child's emotional needs while having high standards. They set limits and are very consistent in enforcing boundaries. Do any of these statements sound like you?

- *You take extra effort to create and maintain a positive relationship with your child.*
- *You clearly explain the reasons for your rules.*
- *You enforce rules and explain its consequences but taking care of your child's feelings.*

If these statements match your behavior, you may be an authoritative parent. Authoritative parents have rules, but they also take their children's opinions into account. They validate their children's feelings, while also making it evident that the adults are ultimately in charge."

Authoritative parenting is said to ultimately be the best parenting style for the child, as it teaches them that there is a balance between love and rules. They have boundaries set for them but understand that boundaries are in place to keep them safe.

An example of this would be telling a child not to touch the stove but explaining that it is because the stove is hot. Children with this parenting style are told no, but in a loving manner with an explanation, so they understand that hearing a no was for their greatest good.

Uninvolved Parenting

Uninvolved parenting is just like what it sounds like, these are parents who don't spend very much time worrying about what their children are doing. You may know that this parenting style as neglect-ful parenting. These are parents who don't think about their children much at all.

According to Wellness Mind,

> *"It is sometimes referred to as neglectful parenting, as the style is characterized by a lack of responsiveness to a child's needs and desires. Uninvolved parents make no demands of their children, and they are often indifferent, or even completely neglectful. Do any of these statements sound familiar?*

> - *You don't ask your kid about school or homework.*
> - *You rarely know where your children are and with whom.*
> - *You don't spend much time with your child.*

> *If those statements sound familiar, you might be an uninvolved parent. Uninvolved parents tend to have little knowledge of what their children are doing. Children may not receive much nurturing, guidance, and parental attention. There tend to be few rules.*

> *Uninvolved parents expect children to raise themselves without much supervision. They do not devote much energy or time into meeting children's basic requirements."*

Children of uninvolved parents may grow up to be very self-sufficient, but also untrusting of love relationships, as their parents did not display very much love or care for them.

One of my friends was a child of neglectful parenting and was left alone for days or weeks at a time as a tween and teen, only having money or food dropped off at infrequent intervals. This type of parenting can harm a child's physical, mental, and emotional well-being.

When small children are neglected, they may be malnourished, delayed learning to walk or talk, and have their growth stunted. They can also lack emotional self-regulation, and basic relationship skills. If babies are neglected, they may even die from the lack of care.

Attachment Parenting

As a parent, I have always prioritized my children's health, safety, and happiness. You could say, we have a child-centered household. If you came to our home, you would see a house that looks like an explosion of toys and art supplies.

When the weekend rolls around, I am apt to be seen taking my kids to a jumpy castle, the rec center or the park. Or, if we are at home, we might all be swimming together, making a craft or watching cartoons all day.

Why do I focus so much of my attention on my kids? Because I subscribe to the philosophy of Attachment Parenting. I know for some people the idea of Attachment Parenting can sound sort of cringeworthy because of what we may have heard in the media, but it is in reality a very science-based approach.

What is Attachment Parenting?

Attachment Parenting, also called **Authoritative Parenting** in the Child Psychology world, is one of four parenting styles outlined in research by Bowlby and Ainsworth. The four parenting styles are Authoritarian, Authoritative, Permissive and Neglectful. These are all based on a continuum of responsiveness and demandingness.

Responsiveness means that the parent responds to the child's needs. Demandingness means that the parent sets high standards for the child. The Authoritative (Attachment) parent is high in both categories.

According to Psychology Today, Attachment Parenting with babies has 4 basic principles:

1. **Co-sleeping** - either in the same room as parents or (with appropriate safety precautions) in the same bed. This may involve having bedtime occur on the child's, not the parent's, schedule.
2. **Feeding on demand** - allowing the child to set the timing of feeding (whether breast- or bottle-fed), along with self-weaning.
3. **Holding and touching** - keeping the child physically near, whether through cuddling and cradling, or by wearing on a front- or backpack arrangement.
4. **Responsiveness to crying** - not letting the child "cry it out," but instead intervening early in the crying bout, reacting to the child's distress before it gets out of control. (The 4 Principles of Attachment Parenting and Why They Work | Psychology Today)

All these principles of Attachment Parenting are important with newborns, because a child forms the attachment to their caregiver by about 6 months of age. A child who is securely attached to their parent or other caregiver will be more successful in other relationships, than children who are not.

As children become older, they will learn to do more things on their own naturally. Children will feel safer to explore the world and try new things when they feel safe and sure in their relationship with their parents. These are children who are confident in knowing that they are loved unconditionally.

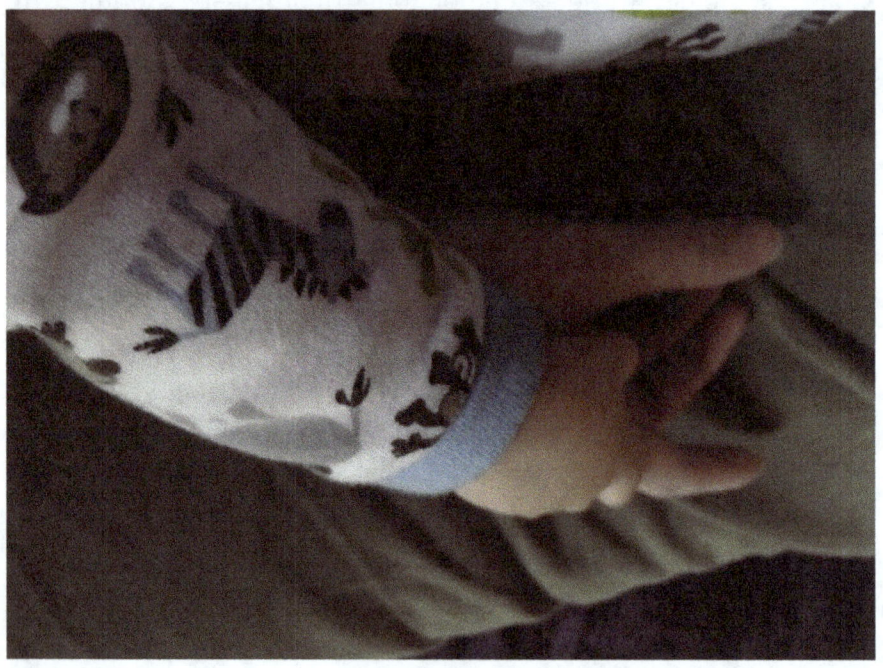

My baby fell asleep holding my hand.

Fulfilling the needs for Love and Safety

By being *responsive* to our children's needs, we help them to build *trust* in the parent-child relationship. Trust that we will always be there when they need us allows children to feel safe. They know that even when they make mistakes, or occasionally disappoint us, we will still love them.

We love our children because of who they are, not what they do.

Conversely, when children feel like they are constantly having to prove themselves to their parents to "earn their love" this can lead to perfectionism, or people pleasing in later relationships. When children are constantly in fear of losing the love and safety of their parental relationships, this can cause a great deal of insecurity and anxiety.

Parents who withhold love from their children create an intrinsic fear in the child that their worth stems only from achievements, and not who they are as a person. This can leave them feeling constantly fearful of other people's opinions, instead of trying to form their own opinions.

The need for safety is one of our most basic as human beings [Maslow's hierarchy of needs], and from an evolutionary perspective we can see this in the fight or flight response.

Small children are dependent on their parents to care for them, and when they can't trust that they will always receive the care they need, they will learn that the world is full of danger. Children who don't feel safe at home can become anxious, because they will have an intensified fight or flight response.

Meeting our children's needs, and making them feel safe, is not spoiling them!

The basic principle behind Attachment Parenting is that the parent becomes a secure base from which the child can move with confidence to explore the world.

Unfortunately, in some circles, fulfilling a child's needs for love and safety is considered spoiling them. We provide for our children's needs for shelter, food, and education without question. Yet when it comes to the need for love and responsiveness, it's ok in the eyes of society for that to be conditional.

Attachment Parenting with Older Children

As children grow older, into elementary school, high school and beyond, their needs change. We can still be responsive to their needs as parents.

We can meet our older children's needs for love and safety, as well as their needs for autonomy and growth. As children get older, we teach them how to problem solve and be more self-sufficient. When this happens, they will need us less and less.

This doesn't mean that they do not need us at all.

Needs of older kids are different. They may need us to help with difficult homework problems or they may need us as a sounding board for problems in relationships with peers and teachers.

Being responsive to these needs doesn't meaning a helicopter parent and following them around to fix all their problems. In the context of an older child or teen, being responsive means creating an environment of openness, where they know, they can talk to us about anything without judgement.

With teens, sometimes being responsive means just being available to listen and let them vent. This is often true of my older daughter, and if she is telling me about a particularly difficult situation, I will ask her if she wants me to do something about it. Often the answer is no. She is more and more able to solve her own problems, she just wants me to be a listening ear and a compassionate heart.

Impact of Attachment on Later Relationships

When children have a healthy and secure relationship with their parents, they are more likely to have healthy relationships later in life. (Bowlby & Ainsworth: What Is Attachment Theory? (verywell-mind.com))

Relationships based on trust are key to our happiness in life.

While looking back at my own childhood experiences, I became aware that my relationships with my parents had created an unhealthy template for my relationships later in life. Basically, because I was alternately abused and neglected by my parents, I had found a relationship with my ex-husband that closely mirrored my relationships with my parents.

Victims of abuse often go from one abusive relationship to another.

After suffering multiple traumas throughout my life, I now have cPTSD (Complex PTSD). I had a low self-image, which made me allow people to treat me badly.

I got into bad relationships because I thought I was a bad person.

Conversely, creating healthy attachments in our relationships with our own children, we can set them up for success later in life. I have strived to create relationships with my children based on care and trust, because it was so badly missing in my own childhood.

Conclusion

After talking about communication skills and their importance to all relationships, as many different important relationships in your life, think about what you may want to work on in your own relationships. Are your relationships typically happy? Or are they tumultuous? What do you think you can do to work on them?

Perhaps you need to work on setting boundaries, or perhaps you need to have some crucial conversations with people in your life. You can use the goal setting worksheets at the back of this book to write about any relationship goals that you may have.

12

Anxiety

If you have tried all of the tips in the previous chapters and are still feeling stressed, it may mean that you have Anxiety. It is still not an insurmountable problem to overcome, but you may want to consult with your healthcare provider.

For years, I have struggled with anxiety without being able to place a name to my feelings. All I knew was, I was stressed and worried all the time. My life was ruled by perpetual fearfulness.

When my toddler was born, I was constantly afraid that she was going to get hurt. I was overwhelmed with constant thoughts that something horrible would happen to her. My incessant fearfulness made me talk to my OBGYN about getting on medication for my postpartum anxiety.

Although I wasn't diagnosed at the time, I believe I had postpartum anxiety with my older daughter as well. When she was a baby, until she was about 9 years old, I was constantly afraid that she was going to get kidnapped. When I went on the hospital tour before she was born, they made a point of telling us that no child had ever been kidnapped from the hospital. After that, I couldn't get the image out of my head.

The upsetting, overpowering worries that I had with each of my children were different, but the constant fear was the same.

I had physical symptoms that accompanied the worries too: heart palpitations, the inability to stop worrying, trouble sleeping, and hyper-awareness. All these are signs of anxiety.

When I had my oldest daughter 18 years ago, Postpartum Anxiety wasn't something I had ever heard of. But 4 years ago, when my toddler was born, there was information readily available online. I also found information in a mom's group that I was a part of and asked my doctor if that could be me.

Do you have anxiety?

If you are feeling anything like I do, it is very possible that you have anxiety. It is estimated that almost 20% of adults in the US experience Anxiety. If you are experiencing any of the following, you may want to talk to your healthcare provider.

Emotional symptoms:

- Feelings of apprehension or dread
- Feeling tense or jumpy
- Restlessness or irritability
- Anticipating the worst and being watchful for signs of danger

Physical symptoms:

- Pounding or racing heart and shortness of breath
- Sweating, tremors, and twitches
- Headaches, fatigue, and insomnia
- Upset stomach, frequent urination, or diarrhea

(Source: https://www.nami.org/About-Mental-Illness/Mental-Health-Conditions/Anxiety-Disorders)

Anxiety is Treatable!

There are treatments available for Anxiety, so if you are struggling with this like I do, have hope that there really is hope at the end of the tunnel. Some of the treatments available are:

- Therapy - with a psychologist or counselor
- Medication - prescribed by a family doctor, psychiatrist or OBGYN
- Complimentary Health Approaches - such as relaxation techniques

(Source: https://www.nami.org/About-Mental-Illness/Mental-Health-Conditions/Anxiety-Disorders)

After struggling with anxiety for years, and having it adversely affect my life since I also have PTSD and depression (which can be common for others with anxiety as well), I finally found a therapy center with ***Wraparound Services.***

Wraparound Services can be super important for anyone who has mental health problems because you get a team of therapists, medical professionals, and advocates to help you navigate the problems with your mental health issues in various aspects of your life.

I love my counseling center because they help me as a team. I got evaluated as a walk-in and had an appointment with a therapist within a week, and a psychiatric nurse within a month. If you have ever had to get a psychiatrist appointment, you know this is quite fast.

My therapist works with me using talk therapy, and coping skills for my daily life. My psychiatric nurse provides me with medications to help with my problems and to alleviate physical anxiety symptoms. My advocate helped me to develop job skills and find employment as a handicapped person. Now, I also see a second therapist who specializes in EMDR for my PTSD.

The best thing about having all these providers in one center?

They all talk to each other, share notes, and provide complimentary services that work together. It is great because I am getting treatment that is consistent from all my providers.

Talk to your doctor today!

If you are struggling with anxiety like me, talk to a doctor today. You can talk to your regular doctor, go to a crisis center, or even go to the ER if it is really a bad day for you. (I have done all of these - and ALL can provide referrals for long-term treatment.)

Coping Strategies.

A big part of my therapy for anxiety has included using coping strategies in my daily life, so that the anxiety doesn't become so overwhelming that I can't function.

Some of these coping strategies include:

- Deep breathing. If you take a breath in, then do a quick and deep exhale, it can calm down your nervous system.
- Meditation. Meditation is also great to practice daily, it helps you learn to quiet your racing thoughts through acceptance.
- Exercise. The endorphins that are released during exercise can help to counteract the fight or flight response from anxiety.
- Yoga. It is a great combination of meditation, exercise and breathing. By learning to make your body flow with your breath, it can create a calm state.
- Journaling. When you are upset and want to yell, it can be great to write things down instead. If you have fears and/or anger, you can release them in a quiet way instead of taking out your feelings on people around you.
- Gratitude. Having a gratitude practice is a great way to flip negative thinking to positive, by shifting your focus to what is going

right already. This can help keep you from thinking about fears of bad things that could happen.

- Affirmations. Like gratitude, this practice of saying positive things to yourself can help to create a more positive mindset as well.

If you, or anyone you know, is considering suicide, please call the National Suicide Prevention Lifeline - 800-273-8255

Please know that you are not alone, and you do not need to suffer in silence anymore!

If you have gone through all the other stress reduction techniques in this book and you are still not feeling better, I would highly recommend consulting with a therapist, to find out if you do have anxiety. As I said in an earlier section, speaking with a therapist and taking medication can go a long way toward lowering your anxiety and helping you to enjoy life again!

13

Conclusion

As we go through life, we can either choose to float along whatever path may be given us or to choose our own path with intention. When we make intentional choices, it allows us to live our best lives. We are going the direction that our heart is leading us to take, instead of simply reacting to circumstances around us.

We make hundreds of choices every day, some more important than others. When we choose a healthy lifestyle full of caring people, activities that we love, and a meaningful job, we can be much happier. Choosing all things that are good for us, in all the elements of our lives, as we discussed in this book can help us to build our best life.

Creating a safe and happy home environment will help you to have a space to do your work, exercise, and play with your kids. You can even decorate your home in ways that help inspire you. Having a comfortable environment can help you to get more done can inspire to rise to your goals.

There are a wide variety of ways to make your life so much happier, and less stressful. Using the techniques in this book can help you become healthier and happier. In the workbook pages to follow, you can outline goals in any of the areas of your life that you want to improve. Whether it is your health, your finances, your relationships, or anything else having a vision is always the place to start. If you haven't already, I encourage you to make a vision board for your perfect life. That way, you always have something inspiring to look at.

Remember, to create real and lasting change in your life, setting goals isn't a one and done process. It is a way of life. Once you meet the goals you set today, you can set new goals and keep continuously improving your life. That is living your best life, constantly making your life better and better, and enjoying the journey mindfully along the way.

References

Stress Management, Mayo Clinic, https://www.mayoclinic.org/healthy-lifestyle/stress-management/in-depth/stress-symptoms/art-20050987

5 Things You Should Know About Stress, National Institute of Mental Health, https://www.nimh.nih.gov/health/publications/stress

The Main Causes of Stress, National Institute of Mental Health, https://www.nimh.nih.gov/health/publications/stress

Use the Wellbeing Model to Reduce Stress, https://www.takingcharge.csh.umn.edu/use-wellbeing-model-reduce-stress

How to Teach Kids to Cope With Stress: The Importance of Resilience, https://www.millenialmom.net/post/can-your-kids-cope-with-stress

Good Health is the Foundation of Happiness, Pritikin, https://www.pritikin.com/your-health/health-foundation-of-happiness.html

The Happiness-Health Connection, Harvard Health, https://www.health.harvard.edu/healthbeat/the-happiness-health-connection

What is Preventative Care?, Health California, https://www.healthforcalifornia.com/blog/what-is-preventive-care#:~:text=Preventive%20care%20can%20help%20keep%20you%20healthy%20longer,to%20start.%20What%20Is%20Included%20in%20Preventive%20Care%3F

How many hours of sleep are enough for good health? Mayo Clinic, https://www.mayoclinic.org/healthy-lifestyle/adult-health/expert-answers/how-many-hours-of-sleep-are-enough/faq-20057898

Put the Phone Away! 3 Reasons Why Looking at It Before Bed Is a Bad Habit, Cleveland Clinic, https://health.clevelandclinic.org/put-the-phone-away-3-reasons-why-looking-at-it-before-bed-is-a-bad-habit/

Here's How Sleep Deprivation Affects Your Productivity, Facile Things, https://facilethings.com/blog/en/sleep-deprivation-and-productivity

Insomnia, WebMD, https://www.webmd.com/sleep-disorders/insomnia-symptoms-and-causes

5 signs you've chosen the right multivitamin, UT Southwestern Medical Center, https://utswmed.org/medblog/multivitamins-supplements/

Make Every Bite Count, Dietary Guidelines for Americans, https://www.dietaryguidelines.gov/

What is the Food Pyramid Now? eMedicineHealth, https://www.emedicinehealth.com/what_is_the_food_pyramid_now/article_em.htm

7 Science-Based Health Benefits of Drinking Enough Water, Healthline, https://www.healthline.com/nutrition/7-health-benefits-of-water

Probiotics, Cleveland Clinic, https://my.clevelandclinic.org/health/articles/14598-probiotics

IBS and Serotonin: The Brain-Stomach Link, Healthline, https://www.healthline.com/health/irritable-bowel-syndrome/serotonin-effects

How much should the average adult exercise every day? Mayo Clinic, https://www.mayoclinic.org/healthy-lifestyle/fitness/expert-answers/exercise/faq-20057916

Walking For Good Health, Victoria Department of Health, https://www.betterhealth.vic.gov.au/health/healthyliving/walking-for-good-health

Mental Benefits of Walking, WebMD, https://www.webmd.com/fitness-exercise/mental-benefits-of-walking#1

What to Know About Walking for Weight Loss, Medical News Today, https://www.medicalnewstoday.com/articles/325809

What are the benefits of sunlight? Healthline, https://www.healthline.com/health/depression/benefits-sunlight

9 Benefits of Yoga, Johns Hopkins Medicine, https://www.healthline.com/health/depression/benefits-sunlight

History of Yoga, Yoga Basics, https://www.yogabasics.com/learn/history-of-yoga/

The Spiritual Side of Yoga – What it Means and How to Achieve it, Himalayan Yoga Institute, https://www.himalayanyogainstitute.com/spiritual-side-yoga-means-achieve/

Spiritual Benefits of Yoga, Best in Yoga, https://bestinyoga.com/spiritual-benefits-of-yoga/

Types of Yoga: A Guide to the Different Styles, Yoga Medicine, https://yogamedicine.com/guide-types-yoga-styles/

What is Mental Health? Mental Health Gov, https://www.mentalhealth.gov/basics/what-is-mental-health

73% of Americans rank their finances as the No. 1 stress in life, according to new Capital One CreditWise survey, CNBC, https://www.cnbc.com/select/73-percent-of-americans-rank-finances-as-the-number-one-stress-in-life/

Credit Report, Annual Credit Report, https://www.annualcreditreport.com/index.action

Credit Report, Credit Karma, https://www.creditkarma.com/

What Is Debt Consolidation, and Should I Consolidate, Nerd Wallet, https://www.nerdwallet.com/article/finance/consolidate-debt

Better Business Bureau, https://www.bbb.org/

3 Steps to Choosing a Qualified Credit Counselor, Nerd Wallet, https://www.nerdwallet.com/article/finance/3-steps-choosing-qualified-credit-counselor

What's the right emergency fund amount? Vanguard, https://investor.vanguard.com/emergency-fund/amount

Savings and Money Market Accounts, Best Rate, https://accounts.bestrates.com/savings-and-money-market-accounts?src=574253&quadlink=http://o1.qnsr.com/cgi/r?;n=203;c=1379980;s=3086;x=7936;f=201303011106180;u=j;z=TIME-STAMP;&ad=396893591939&fb=best%20high%20interest%20savings%20ac-count&mt=e&adposition=&dev=c&network=g&gclid=CjwKCAjw2bm-LBhBREiwAZ6ugo3azjIQKN_1TiCATIMCHQ-OOUCmPf0nnnipcpu-7bZRpaiZYZPvTJRoCt6QQAvD_BwE

Understanding Universal Life Insurance, Forbes Advisor, https://www.forbes.com/advisor/life-insurance/universal-life-insurance/

Best Places to Find Freelance Work Online, The Balance Careers, https://www.thebalancecareers.com/find-freelance-work-online-2072051

5 Reasons to do that hard task early, Inner Drive, https://blog.innerdrive.co.uk/5-reasons-to-do-that-hard-task-early

Benefits and Options for Therapy, Healthline, https://www.healthline.com/health/benefits-of-therapy

Our Top 10 Online Therapy Picks for 2021, Healthline, https://www.healthline.com/health/our-top-10-online-therapy-picks

Less Stress, More Happiness: How Mindfulness Can Combat Stress, Chester County Hospital, https://www.chestercountyhospital.org/news/health-eliving-blog/2021/april/how-mindfulness-can-combat-stress

Getting Started With Mindfulness, Mindful, https://www.mindful.org/meditation/mindfulness-getting-started/

Seven Essential Attitudes of Mindfulness, Mindful Adventure, https://mindfuladventure.com/mindfulness-2/seven-essential-attitudes-of-mindfulness/

Practice Mindful Parenting, Child Mind Institute, https://childmind.org/article/mindful-parenting-2/

Meditation: A simple, fast way to reduce stress, The Mayo Clinic, https://www.mayoclinic.org/tests-procedures/meditation/in-depth/meditation/art-20045858

The Many Benefits of Meditation, Headspace, https://www.headspace.com/meditation/benefits

How to Meditate, Headspace, https://www.headspace.com/meditation/how-to-meditate

Which Type of Meditation Is Right for Me? Healthline, https://www.healthline.com/health/mental-health/types-of-meditation#overview

Purposeful activity – hobbies, Head to Health, https://www.headtohealth.gov.au/meaningful-life/purposeful-activity/hobbies

How to Practice Active Listening, Very Well Mind, https://www.verywellmind.com/what-is-active-listening-3024343

Transformational Listening, Dr. Robin Johnson, https://drrobinjohnson.com/listening/

Why Personal Boundaries are Important and How to Set Them, Psych Central, https://psychcentral.com/lib/what-are-personal-boundaries-how-do-i-get-some

The No BS Guide to Protecting Your Emotional Space, Healthline, https://www.healthline.com/health/mental-health/set-boundaries

Do Relationships Make Us Healthier and Happier? Psychology Today, https://www.psychologytoday.com/us/blog/the-mindful-self-express/201612/do-relationships-make-us-healthier-and-happier

How does Love Affect Happiness? Psychology Today, https://www.psychologytoday.com/us/blog/the-mysteries-love/201503/how-does-love-affect-happiness

What to Know About Premarital Counseling, The Knot, https://www.theknot.com/content/premarital-counseling

Does Marriage Make Us Happy? American Psychological Association, https://www.apa.org/monitor/2010/10/marriage

The best advice for a healthy marriage, Health Prep, https://healthprep.com/family-pregnancy/healthy-marriage-advice/?utm_source=bing&utm_medium=search&utm_campaign=370437812&utm_content=1274334659236701&utm_term=about%20marriage&msclkid=b4ada3f1c045160d1af0c28145cb909f

4 Types of Parenting Styles and Their Effects on Kids, Wellness Mind, https://wellnessmind.org/4-types-of-parenting-styles/

The 4 Principles of Attachment Parenting and Why They Work, Psychology Today, https://www.psychologytoday.com/us/blog/fulfillment-any-age/201307/the-4-principles-attachment-parenting-and-why-they-work

What Is Attachment Theory? Very Well Mind, https://www.verywellmind.com/what-is-attachment-theory-2795337

Anxiety Disorders, National Alliance on Mental Illness, https://www.nami.org/About-Mental-Illness/Mental-Health-Conditions/Anxiety-Disorders

Additional Planning Worksheets

On the following pages, you will find additional Goal Planning and Budget Planning worksheets, so that you can write your goals and budget as many times as you need! It can be helpful to have goals in all different areas of your life. You can also make additional copies as needed.

Mission and Values

Personal Values and Mission Statement:

Work Goals:

Affirmations:

Life Goals

Personal Goals:

Work Goals:

Family Goals:

Action Steps

Personal Goals:

Work Goals:

Family Goals:

Weekly Goals

Personal Goals:

Work Goals:

Family Goals:

Daily Goals

Personal Goals:

Work Goals:

Family Goals:

Mission and Values

Personal Values and Mission Statement:

Work Goals:

Affirmations:

Life Goals

Personal Goals:

Work Goals:

Family Goals:

Action Steps

Personal Goals:

Work Goals:

Family Goals:

Weekly Goals

Personal Goals:

Work Goals:

Family Goals:

Daily Goals

Personal Goals:

Work Goals:

Family Goals:

Mission and Values

Personal Values and Mission Statement:

Work Goals:

Affirmations:

Life Goals

Personal Goals:

Work Goals:

Family Goals:

Action Steps

Personal Goals:

Work Goals:

Family Goals:

Weekly Goals

Personal Goals:

Work Goals:

Family Goals:

Daily Goals

Personal Goals:

Work Goals:

Family Goals:

Income	Anticipated Amount	Actual Amount	Date	
In Savings				
Payroll				
Other Income				
Total	0	0		

Expenses	Minimum Payment	Actual Payment	Date Due	Date Paid
Mortgage				
Water				
Sewer				
Trash				
Electric				
Savings				
Credit Card				
Student Loans				

Total	0	0		
Remaining Balance	0	0		

Income	Anticipated Amount	Actual Amount	Date	
In Savings				
Payroll				
Other Income				
Total	0	0		

Expenses	Minimum Payment	Actual Payment	Date Due	Date Paid
Mortgage				
Water				
Sewer				
Trash				
Electric				
Savings				
Credit Card				
Student Loans				

Total	0	0	
Remaining Balance	0	0	

Income	Anticipated Amount	Actual Amount	Date	
In Savings				
Payroll				
Other Income				
Total	0	0		

Expenses	Minimum Payment	Actual Payment	Date Due	Date Paid
Mortgage				
Water				
Sewer				
Trash				
Electric				
Savings				
Credit Card				

Student Loans				
Total	0	0		
Remaining Balance	0	0		

Income	Anticipated Amount	Actual Amount	Date	
In Savings				
Payroll				
Other Income				
Total	0	0		

Expenses	Minimum Payment	Actual Payment	Date Due	Date Paid
Mortgage				
Water				
Sewer				
Trash				
Electric				
Savings				
Credit Card				
Student Loans				

Total	0	0		
Remaining Balance	0	0		

Income	Anticipated Amount	Actual Amount	Date	
In Savings				
Payroll				
Other Income				
Total	0	0		

Expenses	Minimum Payment	Actual Payment	Date Due	Date Paid
Mortgage				
Water				
Sewer				
Trash				
Electric				
Savings				
Credit Card				
Student Loans				

Total	0	0	
Remaining Balance	0	0	

Income	Anticipated Amount	Actual Amount	Date	
In Savings				
Payroll				
Other Income				
Total	0	0		

Expenses	Minimum Payment	Actual Payment	Date Due	Date Paid
Mortgage				
Water				
Sewer				
Trash				
Electric				
Savings				
Credit Card				

Student Loans				
Total	0	0		
Remaining Balance	0	0		

www.ingramcontent.com/pod-product-compliance
Lightning Source LLC
Chambersburg PA
CBHW060510130626
46553CB00002B/444